Metacritique

Metacritique

The philosophical argument of Jürgen Habermas

GARBIS KORTIAN

TRANSLATED BY JOHN RAFFAN
WITH AN INTRODUCTORY ESSAY BY
CHARLES TAYLOR AND ALAN MONTEFIORE

CAMBRIDGE UNIVERSITY PRESS

CAMBRIDGE
LONDON · NEW YORK · NEW ROCHELLE
MELBOURNE · SYDNEY

Published by the Press Syndicate of the University of Cambridge
The Pitt Building, Trumpington Street, Cambridge CB2 1RP
32 East 57th Street, New York, NY 10022, USA
296 Beaconsfield Parade, Middle Park, Melbourne 3206, Australia

First published 1980

Set, printed and bound in Great Britain by
Fakenham Press Limited, Fakenham, Norfolk

British Library Cataloguing in Publication Data
Kortian, Garbis
Metacritique.
1. Habermas, Jürgen
I. Title
193   B3258.H324   79–42798

ISBN 0 521 22374 1 hard covers
ISBN 0 521 29618 8 paperback

To my Mother

Contents

From an analytical perspective

The outstanding feature of the interpretation of Habermas that Garbis Kortian offers to the English-speaking reader in this book lies in the way in which he situates Habermas's enterprise in relation to its philosophical background, tracing its roots in classical German Idealism, and in particular in Hegel's critique of Kant and in the subsequent transformation of this critique by Marx.

If it is to be taken on its own terms, this, surely, is the only way in which the enterprise of critical theory can be properly understood. Habermas himself lays out his position, in the global statement that he offers in *Erkenntnis und Interesse*, by means of a critique of, among others, Kant, Fichte, Hegel and Marx. His own work thus constitutes an attempt to redefine and to carry forward an enterprise which has been going on in European philosophy for nearly two centuries and which has been among the formative ideas of our culture as we now have it.

Notoriously, however, this enterprise has been little appreciated or even understood in Anglo-Saxon philosophy of the last half-century or so; indeed, it has been only rather sporadically represented in English-language culture during the last century and a half. This inevitably makes it difficult for someone from within this culture to gain a familiar sense of the ground-plan of the house of critical theory, a house which is continually being reconstructed through the different variations which the theory undergoes; and this absence of any sense of a ground-plan may make the discussions hard to follow.

And yet the philosophical traditions which run through Hegel have the same roots as those with which the contemporary Anglo-Saxon world is more familiar. We share as sources not only the ancients, but also the Enlightenment and Kant – or Descartes, Hume and Kant, to put it in terms of the usual university syllabus. It should, therefore, be possible to complement Dr Kortian's achievements in exhibiting so convincingly the relation of Habermas's thought to Hegel's critique of Kant by situating this critique in a context already more familiar to readers of English-language philosophy. This, at any rate, is what we attempt in this brief introductory essay.

We may start with one of the central themes of Dr Kortian's book: Hegel's critique of the epistemological enterprise which dominates modern philosophy from Descartes onwards. In this respect the experiences of the two major philosophical traditions, the German and the Anglo-Saxon, have been very different. First, the very terms of epistemological debate underwent fundamental revision at the hands of Kant; and then Hegel aimed at the whole enterprise a blow which was meant to be fatal. In fact, in neither culture did it just lie down and die. For example, it was in different ways central to the preoccupations of the neo-Kantians, of Brentano, of the early Husserl and of Mach, to name but a few of those working in the German-speaking world at the turn of the century. Nevertheless, the long-term effect of the Hegelian critique has been to displace epistemology as the organising discipline of thought and the questions to which it gives rise in the German-speaking world. That this is so would be common ground between philosophers of such very different tendencies as, for example, Marxists, Heideggerians, critical theorists, etc.

In the Anglo-Saxon world, by contrast, epistemology was a much longer time a-dying. Until recently, there was a still very lively interest in a widely-held form of sense-data theory, which, it might be argued, was oblivious even of the Kantian critique, let alone of any accounts it had to render to

Hegel. Indeed, it is probably more correct to say that it is not yet dead at all; that for many philosophers epistemological questions go on playing the organising role; that the questions of what there is, of what we can say, of the nature of man, of language, etc., go on being framed so as to fit in with certain answers to the question of what it is to know. This is the case for those philosophers, for instance, for whom the natural sciences remain paradigmatic of human knowledge and even rationality itself; among such philosophers one might surely place such distinguished figures as Popper and Quine – despite the latter's repudiation of traditional epistemology as a foundational enterprise.

Moreover, where epistemology has been dethroned in the Anglo-Saxon world, it is under the impact of quite different arguments from those of Hegel. Here the major force has perhaps been that of the later Wittgenstein, whose undermining of certain dogmas of the epistemological approach has been immensely influential. But Wittgenstein's critique is so different from Hegel's that it provides little help in making it more accessible or more intelligible.

Perhaps, therefore, the most useful point at which to start would be with a sketch of this Hegelian critique of epistemology, a critique which is only tersely expressed in his *Phenomenology of Spirit*, but which is central to his work.

Epistemology, as we know it since Descartes, involves an attempt to test our knowledge claims and to get clear which of them are really well-grounded and which are specious. The aim is to establish the foundations of knowledge; the search is for that on which our claims may be given a secure basis. If all goes well, the search for foundations will come across basic elements or components which cannot further be broken down or seen to be grounded on something else. At that point everything will turn on how certain we can be of them; or on just what it may be that we know for certain if and when we possess them. For the empiricists, of course, it was the ideas or impressions of conscious subjective experience that played the role of such basic components.

Epistemology conceived in this way seemed to be an enterprise that it was rational to pursue not only for its own sake, but also as providing an indispensable foundation for philosophy itself. For how could any other inquiry – metaphysics, ontology or anthropology – be pursued independently of epistemology? In all these fields we seek valid knowledge claims; and we cannot even know what these may be until we have determined what it is to have properly founded knowledge. The findings of all other inquiries have thus to pass muster according to the canons laid down in epistemology; and it is epistemology which can, therefore, help us to understand something of the form which any successful inquiry must take.

This standard and highly persuasive line of argument has had an immense influence on our culture. In its name, for instance, our sciences of man have been conceived very largely on the model of those of nature, in defiance indeed of many of the intuitions that we have as ordinary men and women. And it is a line of thought which continues to be very persuasive.

It is this line of thought that Hegel's arguments were meant to kill off once and for all. Hegel's point can perhaps be reconstructed in these terms. The epistemological project may sound very legitimate when put in quite general terms, but in order to carry it out, one has to rest it on a number of assumptions. For instance, one needs some idea of what it can *be* to ground one knowledge claim on other more basic ones, of what a basic knowledge claim could actually be. Otherwise, we are in turn in no proper position to ask such questions as: how certain is this or that claim? how certain are our basic claims? what do we know for certain? etc. etc. But, within the epistemological tradition, these crucial assumptions, which necessarily depend on the adoption of some view of the subject and his place in the world, are all made surreptitiously, without recognition of what is involved.

We may take classical empiricism as a prime example.

This was not in fact the target which Hegel has mainly in mind; as Dr Kortian says, his critique was directed above all at Kant. But empiricism is most familiar to philosophers in our culture. Here there was an unchallenged notion of what factual knowledge claims were based upon, namely, sense experience; and there was a definite conception of what this sense experience was like. It consisted of what Hume called 'impressions' or of what have latterly been called 'sense-data' – the conscious contents of immediately present awareness. From this firm base, it seemed unquestioningly possible to pose problems as to the status of our knowledge claims about, for example, the links between cause and effect; one had simply to ask how, if at all, they were grounded in impressions. Thanks to these assumptions as to the nature of experience, the question had an answerable form.

But no one ever asked what justified the assumptions themselves. In fact, they were based on some insufficiently articulated view of the subject's position in the world, a subject conceived as a mind somehow affected by the action of objects in contact with the sense organs belonging to the body with which this mind was in some way linked. 'Impressions' were taken to constitute the most basic elements of experience. We could know them for what they were independently of any other knowledge or assumptions; the rest of our knowledge was indeed to be grounded upon them. Yet the very use of the term 'impression' says a great deal about this view through the image that it contains: the things of the world somehow make their impress on the senses and through them on the mind – and it is in this way that we can come to know things.

Granted such a view of the basic building blocks of perception, one could hope to answer questions about, for instance, the status of causal attribution. Within his own terms, Hume's answer was surely right. If we think of visual space and ask what separate impression may correspond to a distinct experience of power or causal efficacy binding two events together, we have to reply that there is none. We can understand that a red billiard ball will make a different impression from a blue one; but how can we understand the idea that when A's motion causes B's motion, it makes a different visual impression from that of B's motion simply following upon that of A?

But these arguments rest on sand – unless one can somehow establish the validity of this underlying view of the mind and of experience. In fact it appears to rest on very shaky assumptions. Quite apart from its own internal (and by this time well known) difficulties, it flies in the face of our phenomenological grasp of our own experience. The one obvious advantage it has is a certain commonsense view of what a scientific understanding of perception might, or perhaps must, be – a view then and now applied without much questioning of the relevance that such an account might have for our understanding of experience.

However, the real point at issue is not whether the empiricist anthropology is well or badly supported, but rather that the (unavoidable) need to have recourse to any such assumptions undercuts the whole epistemological enterprise. For this enterprise aims at evaluating our knowledge claims by showing what they are founded on and what the foundations truly establish. But it turns out that the enterprise can only get going on the basis of massive assumptions about the nature of experience, which means in effect about the nature of mind and its place in nature. These assumptions, however, cannot be tested by the canons of epistemology, for they have to be held steady for the very enterprise of generating these canons to get under way.

But these assumptions, far from being unproblematic and commonsensical, are highly conjectural and bound up with very controversial theory. Epistemology as a foundational enterprise is thus hopelessly compromised. It cannot after all lay down the law to other branches of inquiry, since it has itself to presuppose certain views in metaphysics and anthropology in order to get going. And indeed it begins to look pretty absurd. The epistemologist arrogates to himself the right to pass judgement on the well-foundedness of all knowledge claims, even to the point of judging very severely our common claims to know that there are physical objects before us, or that we are conversing with other conscious beings like ourselves, while in fact his own enterprise and claims are grounded on certain highly conjectural and controversial assumptions. One short answer to Humean epistemology is that we can all be much more certain of the causal link between the player's kick and the goal, between my neighbour's bad driving and the dent in my bumper, than that our experience consists 'at bottom' of (essentially incorrigible) impressions. The absurdity of classical empiricism is that it contrives to make it appear as though the reverse were the case.

Hegel's arguments in the introduction to the *Phenomenology of Spirit*, where he takes as his examples conceptions of the knowing faculty as an instrument or as a medium, were meant to show the impossibility in principle of epistemology as a foundational enterprise. The very idea of making a critique of knowledge claims from the secure base of some in itself unproblematic notion of experience was in principle mistaken. Any critique has to be directed rather at a whole package: knowledge-claim-cum-view-of-the-object-or-elements-of experience. This is a conclusion on which none of those who stand in the tradition which runs from Hegel through Marx to critical theory have wanted to go back. The 'metacritical dimension' of Hegel's thought, as Dr Kortian calls it, is a basic point of reference for this whole school of thought. This is one of the things that may make it strange for an English-language philosopher.

Of course, the argument in its original Hegelian form is mainly directed at a Kantian target. This may seem somewhat unfair in the light of the above discussion, since some of Kant's most important arguments are directed by his rejection of some of the basic assumptions of the empiricist (and, ultimately, Cartesian) concept of experience. At the same time, however, he kept a great deal of the basic structure of thought which came to him from the epistemological tradition in which, after all, he still stood as one of its greatest figures. Most notably, he continued to struggle with the notion of a subject affected in some way or another by a realm of things outside it and whose experience has hence to be understood as made up of 'representations'; and so on. He in no way questions the epistemological enterprise as such. Hegel's arguments thus represent a far more radical critique, which, following the precedent of Hamann and Herder (whose attacks on Kant certainly influenced Hegel), we can call a 'metacritique'.

Nevertheless, although originally directed against Kant, the general anti-epistemological argument clearly weighs against empiricism and positivism as well, in particular against the tendency to extract certain paradigms of knowledge from the natural sciences and to treat them as normative for all knowledge, even for rationality as such. This is a tendency which critical theory in our day has repeatedly attacked as a form of thought thrown up by the needs and presuppositions of technological, bureaucratic and, characteristically, capitalist society, a facet of its ideological self-understanding. The claim, like that of Hegel, is that this apparent certainty about the nature of knowledge is grounded on unself-critical assumptions about the nature of the subject and his relation to others and to his world. The supposedly firm foundations of these notions of science and rationality are in reality a sham.

But although this Hegelian 'metacritique' is a reference point for the whole critical tradition, it has been developed in quite different ways. Hegel's way of conceiving it in the *Phenomenology of Spirit* was vigorously criticised by Marx; and this critique too has been taken up by critical theory.

These differences may be brought out if we start by asking where one can go once one realises the ultimate inadequacy of the merely epistemological approach. One has then critically to weigh whole packages of knowledge claims taken along with views as to the nature of the knowing (but no longer merely knowing) subject, views of what is or can be known along with views of what it is to know, of the 'criterion' (*Masstab*) of knowledge. The question, then, is: how is one to go about criticising these packages?

It would be understandable, indeed, were one to throw up one's hands in despair and settle for a purely sceptical conclusion. If the very criticism of knowledge depends itself on highly speculative assumptions, then clearly nothing can be firmly grounded, and we can never 'know' which of two fundamentally conflicting views is right.

Hegel proposes a way out of this difficulty, the path of what later came to be called 'immanent critique'. For packages can be criticised on their own terms, tested for their consistency to see whether what they recognise as knowledge is consistent with their own conception of the subject and of what knowledge consists in. If they fail to hold together in this way, then they refute themselves, and on their own terms. There is no need to refer outside them to some external standpoint or criterion to see that they are inadequate.

Hegel starts the dialectic of the *Phenomenology of Spirit* by bringing to light the inconsistency of our common conceptions of the subject and of knowledge. These, he argues, cannot in fact stand up to systematic examination. Although Hegel does not here go into them, there are certain general reasons why we should expect that an unsystematic or erroneous package will not stand up. For we have to render consistent our view of the subject and its, his or her position in the world (and hence our view of what subjective experience is) with our conception of the role of (subjective) experience in our knowledge of an (objective) world. And this has to be done in the light of what we recognise as criterial properties of experience and knowledge – for example, those explored by Kant in his Transcendental Deduction, namely that experience must be of an object and must be minimally coherent, or else that invoked by Hegel in the first chapter of the *Phenomenology of Spirit*, namely that we must be able to say what we are certain of. All this constitutes a major task; it would be an equally major achievement if we succeeded in elaborating a single overall view capable of overcoming all the tensions and inconsistencies between our conceptions of experience and its psychology and of what it is to acquire knowledge. Certainly, classical empiricism fails to achieve any such consistency, since while claiming to found all our knowledge of independently existing objects on sensa, of which allegedly we can be certain in a way that we cannot be of the objects themselves, it nevertheless assumes that we are, as embodied beings, sensory objects among objects, receiving sensory input from the things around us. The framework of the material universe surrounding us is already assumed in the supposed reconstruction of knowledge from sensa alone. There is in this way something incoherent in the very idea of such a reconstruction, indeed in the very idea of a sensum, or 'impression', as an epistemologically fundamental item.

But if 'immanent critique' can show the inadequacy of our ordinary conceptions, does this not still leave us in a predicament not very different from that described by sceptics, that is to say in a position in which we can tell that we are wrong but can never know what is right?

Hegel claims not. For in each case the contradiction or inconsistency involved in any particular package takes a quite definite form. There is thus some specific inadequacy to be made up. The method of immanent critique shows us not only *that* a given package or view is wrong, but also *how* it is wrong. In this way, it indicates the possibility of an amended view, altered to take account of the now exposed inadequacy. Of course, this amended view is likely to have its own inadequacy, and so require further amendment. Thus the prospect opens up of a chain of arguments, in which our ordinary conceptions of the subject and of experience are progressively criticised and amended, until we may reach a conclusion in a conception which could at last stand up as no longer inconsistent with itself.

This path of alternating criticism and amendment is the 'dialectical' way of the *Phenomenology of Spirit*, where each position establishes itself as superior to its predecessor purely through the force of argument. But this is where the criticism of Hegel by Marx and those inspired by him arises. This criticism is directed not just against the final terminus of Hegel's argument – that is, against a supposed 'absolute knowledge' in which subject and object are no longer separated, and in which knowledge and self-knowledge are one and the same. This conception is, of course, unacceptable from a materialist standpoint, since it implies that men as finite, natural beings are somehow united to an infinite subject. But criticism is also directed against Hegel's very manner of proceeding as based, say the critics, on a crucial misunderstanding of what is involved in erroneous conceptions of subject, experience and knowledge; for these, so it is argued, are never merely intellectual errors, but have their roots in the social and material forms of life of the subject.

Thus, according to this line of argument, and to take classical empiricism once again as an example, the conception that knowledge starts with the passive reception of the data of the senses, and, moreover, the passive reception of such data by an individual or epistemologically self-sufficient subject, will seem overwhelmingly plausible in a society in which, effectively, men are functioning as atomic individuals – that is, in a society whose rules, institutions and constitutive practices define men as self-determined but essentially interchangeable individuals, and in which, consequently, they have lost sight of the way in which the objects they have to deal with are shaped by social labour. On this view, critical theory cannot be content just to show how, for example, classical empiricism is inconsistent or that its conception of the subject must be wrong because it leads to contradictions. If we seek to proceed to a more adequate conception, we have to go on to explain what made the inadequate one seem so plausible in its time and context; we have to identify the element of truth that it contains, to show in what ways it really does reflect life in an atomised society, if we are to identify what is false in it and needs to be changed in order to arrive at a more adequate conception. The theoretical contradiction that lies within its view of the subject and experience has to be followed down to its root, which is to be found in a practical contradiction in a form of social life, a contradiction which can only function by denying its own foundations in social labour. It is only at this point that one can adequately understand the contradiction; only when one adequately understands it can one hope to resolve it and to postulate a successor stage, a new conception rooted in a new form of social life and free at least of the inconsistencies characteristic of its predecessor.

In this new form of social life – so the argument continues – a fuller, more adequate conception of both subject and experience would be our normal self-understanding. Indeed, we might say that if present social reality tends to mask from us the nature of our own social (reality) activity, constantly leading us to see ourselves as atomic individuals with passively receptive minds, then we shall be in a position properly to grasp a new, fuller conception of ourselves only when we have transformed our present society. We may perhaps already have some idea of its general outlines, but we cannot hope properly to understand how to state it until we live in a different social reality.

By this time the Hegelian dialectic has taken on a quite different aspect. It is no longer just a matter of showing up contradictions in our conceptions of the subject, of experience and of knowledge, of amending them in order to resolve the contradictions and of then repeating the process with the amended forms. Rather, properly to show the contradiction in the conception involves now tracing its roots in social reality; hence, the task of elaborating a new, more adequate conception involves changing this reality. In this way, we arrive at a metacritique not just of conceptions of the subject, but at the same time of forms of social reality; we have a theory which is at once an explanation for the inadequacy of our views and a guide for transforming reality. Or, as Habermas puts it, the theory gives an account both of the context in which it itself arises (its *Entstehungszusammenhang*), along with all the inadequacies of existing conceptions and reality, and of its context of effective application (its *Verwendungszusammenhang*) as a guide for changing what exists (cf. p. 46).

This is different from Hegel's procedure – though it must in all fairness be said that he was far from oblivious of the social dimensions of our conceptions of subject and knowledge. It was not at all that, as some Marxists have implied, Hegel thought that one could have a dialectic of pure thought forms succeeding one another without a corresponding dialectic of social forms following upon one another in history. The real difference of method comes rather from a very different view of the place of the reflecting subject in this whole process.

For Hegel, the full self-awareness of the reflective subject comes only at the end of a whole series of moves from less to more adequate forms of (self-) consciousness and after the historical transformations of society which have made it possible. Philosophy only arrives at a retrospective understanding; in the famous image of the preface to the *Philosophy of Right*, the owl of Minerva flies only at dusk. Hegel is very far from believing that there are no social conditions necessary for adequate self-understanding. But he sees this self-understanding as a kind of recapitulation arrived at only after the historically necessary conditions have come about. Clear self-understanding can have no revolutionary implications if only because we cannot achieve clarity in our understanding of ourselves until after the revolution has taken place.

For Marx, on the other hand, this self-understanding is itself part of the process of revolutionary transformation. Indeed, the transition to socialism presupposes a certain self-understanding on the part of the class which brings it about; the proletariat must have a grasp of scientific socialism. If, in the revolutionary predicament described by Marx, the serenely recapitulative reflection of the *Phenomenology of Spirit* seems bloodless and irrelevant, this is not because it ignores the question of its social foundations. On the contrary, the *Phenomenology of Spirit* is very much aware of them, and the social forms which have been the matrices of our self-understanding also have their place in the recapitulation. It is rather that the 'real' historical, social transformations relevant to this self-understanding are seen as already effected. For Hegel, thought must reconcile us to a rational reality; for Marx, it has to unmask existent irrationality and guide its transformation.

Of course, this difference in the role of (self-) reflection is bound up with the fundamental differences between the two thinkers' conceptions of history, and above all with the one's focus on Spirit and the other's focus on Man. To trace out these differences would take us too far afield; the immediate point is simply that Hegel had not merely ignored the social dimension of the dialectic, but rather conceived it very differently.

In any case, one of the great merits of Garbis Kortian's book lies in the way in which he places Habermas and the critical school firmly within the tradition which is defined by Hegel's metacritique of epistemology and Marx's subsequent transformation of this into a social critique. Evidently, and most importantly, once one has made this second step, one has displaced the whole centre of gravity of the critique, and it no longer has to start as a critique of epistemology. The critique of class society can just as well start from the insoluble conflicts of practical reason which it claims to articulate for us; for example, the contradictions inherent in our atomist models of freedom, or those between promised enrichment and real impoverishment, between promised influence or efficacy and real powerlessness, and so on.

It is thus easy to mistake or even to forget the roots of all this in the Hegelian critique, and indeed in the terms of that epistemological debate – the 'subject' and its relation to its world of experience – against which that critique was primarily directed. And yet an understanding of these roots is essential to our understanding of this kind of thinking. It only makes sense to talk of society as being in contradiction with itself, rather than as just being in conflict or as suffering 'malfunction' in terms of some criterion essentially external to it, if one sees certain conceptions of the social agent and his purposes as integral to or as partly constitutive of social reality. We can properly speak of a contradiction in bourgeois freedom, if we see the negation of the freedom which is *in principle* central to the institutions of bourgeois society as being inevitable in the actual practice of this society. Of course, if we do not see a reference to freedom as a fundamental value as essential to the proper characterisation of bourgeois society and its institutions, but simply as one among a number of demands that as a matter of contingent fact we make upon them, then the absence of freedom will appear merely as a malfunction relative to this particular demand and not as a true contradiction, as a 'disvalue' in terms of our own subjective standards rather than as a feature crucial to our understanding of the ways in which it functions in practice.

Thus, a critical Marxism must always operate at two levels, identifying both the contradictions in our conceptions and aspirations and their roots in the underlying social reality. If it tries to abandon the first level and to develop a 'science' of society which would make no reference to conceptions and aspirations as integral to or partially constitutive of our institutions, then it becomes just another would-be positive science, offering a value-free account of society to which we could each bring our own evaluative demands; and in so doing, it falls victim to the epistemological mould of thought so effectively criticised by Hegel.

This is a fate which constantly threatens one leading

strand of Marxist thought, which takes our standard contemporary view of natural science as paradigmatic for its
own understanding of history. This strand derives, no doubt,
from certain formulations of Marx and Engels themselves.
Indeed, this is the ground of Habermas's critique of Marx in
Erkenntnis und Interesse. And Habermas himself develops the
other strand, the strand of immanent critique of social reality.

But this kind of thinking is only possible if we keep alive
the requirements of immanent critique as originally laid
down by Hegel. It requires above all that we remain constantly aware of how our own thinking about a distorted
social reality can itself be distorted by this reality. This was,
after all, the original insight of critical Marxism, that the
inconsistencies of the empiricist conception were not just a
gratuitous error, but were motivated or made plausible by
the prevailing social conditions. It is not possible simply to
set aside or by-pass this error so long as those conditions
exist.

This means that the critique of epistemology cannot just
be made once and for all and then left behind as finished
business, as data for historians of the subject. To allow this
critique to be forgotten on the grounds that it has been
already accomplished is simply to risk falling victim once
again to the same epistemological illusion, an illusion constantly regenerated by the conditions in which we live. This,
to simplify a little, is, in Habermas's view, one of the misfor-
tunes which befell mainstream Marxism. At times Marx
himself seemed to believe, or at least half-believe, that once
the critique of philosophy was made, it could be set aside,
and we could embark on a positive science of society which
did not incorporate this critique as one of its foundations,
but, at most, as an off-shoot, in a subordinate, special theory
of ideology. But, as Habermas would argue, to embark on a
'positive' science of society in this civilisation is to take on all
the unreflected notions, stemming from the epistemological
tradition, which are at its root. It is, in effect, to take on once

more the unreflected conception of the passive subject in a world of objects. All this is so inconsistent with some of the main insights of Marxism that it is not surprising that the resulting 'science' should present a very strange mixture, full of crudities and *non sequiturs*, as one can see in examining, for example, official Soviet Marxism or at least the earlier versions of Althusser's interpretation.

Thus, for Habermas the renewal of critical theory has necessarily involved the renewal of its links with the critique of epistemology, and this in turn has required a retracing of its roots in Kant and Hegel. In the course of this reformulation, he has developed some extremely interesting and fruitful ideas which Dr Kortian sketches out in this book, but which, as Kortian also indicates, would repay much further working out, further even than Habermas himself has yet managed to achieve.

Thus, he renews the critique of epistemology with the development of the notion of a plurality of 'interests' serving as the motivations for the acquisition of knowledge in different domains. These are conceived not simply as the *de facto* motivations of particular research groups, but, rather, as contributing towards a definition of the life of the subject in the context of which the criteria of successful knowledge claims are established. Habermas's inquiry into interests is a transcendental inquiry. With this conception of a plurality of interests, he tries to break loose from the assumption of the classical epistemological condition that all knowledge claims are to be understood on the basis of a single model. There are interesting parallels here with a number of analytic philosophers, for example Stephen Toulmin; or with Wittgenstein's attempt to shatter the single-model 'theory' of meaning by introducing the notion of a plurality of language games.

At the same time Habermas is trying to open up a quite new dimension of immanent critique with a theory of language designed to show that the very use of language presupposes a context of communication which, although empirically always imperfect, points to an ideal context of communication free from all distortion and constraint. In other words, speech activity itself is seen as based on certain standards which allow us to recognise the distortions in our present forms of communication for what they are.

This theory, if developed further, might provide one of the most powerful and penetrating avenues of social criticism and could set the tradition in which it stands on a new path. Its author is certainly one of the most original and fertile of contemporary philosophers.

But to understand his thought, one has to place it in the tradition we have been discussing, as he himself does, and as Garbis Kortian so well explains in this book. The difficulty is that this tradition is so little available, or accessible only with difficulty, to philosophers trained in the Anglo-Saxon world.

This tradition can perhaps be best identified by reference to the two main steps we have outlined here, the Hegelian metacritique of epistemology and its Marxist reformulation as social critique. Behind them, of course, stands the giant figure of Kant with his deep and difficult theory of the knowing and acting subject's constitutive relationship with the world both as object for its knowledge and as context for its action. Kant is once again relatively familiar to thinkers in our culture; but Hegel and Marx are still relatively much less so. This is, no doubt, partly due to the fact that the primacy of epistemology is not so much a thing of the past in the English-speaking world as it is on much of the continent of Europe – in the Anglo-Saxon world Kant has been studied much more exclusively in terms of his epistemology; and partly because the critique of epistemology, where it has taken place, has tended to take a quite different form.

The major attack on the epistemological tradition in our philosophical culture comes in the arguments of the later Wittgenstein. Wittgenstein does indeed show that the conception of experience and of the meaning of words implicit in this tradition is close to untenable. But he does this by showing that it renders much of our linguistic practice unintelligible. In this his attack runs partially parallel to Kant's attack on what may be called Cartesian (including, most notably, classical empiricist) epistemology, in which Kant showed that the conception of experience fundamental to this epistemology was unable to account for experience as a genuinely recognisable possibility. In the one case experience, in the other the practice of language, are shown to be impossible on the Cartesian construction.

The doctrines are shown to be wrong, but there is no attempt at proof that the enterprise which gave rise to these doctrines is incoherent and needs to be replaced by a quite different one. Kant, indeed, whatever else he may have been, and however profound the modifications he may have introduced in the notions of subject, object and experience, was still a very major epistemologist. In Wittgenstein, indeed, there is a strong suggestion that the epistemological enterprise is based on a fundamental mistake; the key notion of certainty could not have one fundamental meaning, a meaning which was not relative to any language game and which the notion must have if the primacy of epistemology is to make sense. For the very enterprise involves ignoring most of the differences of contexts in which the word plays different roles, and thus generating the puzzles and confusions that are so typical of philosophy.

This is a powerful refutation of epistemology as a foundational enterprise, as powerful in its own way as the Hegelian. But it points in a quite different direction. Foundational epistemology is mistaken in principle because our ordinary speech is all right as it is, and the project to reconstruct it in some canonical form is gratuitous and based on a misunderstanding. What ought to take its place is not, therefore, another, more radically critical theory, as follows in the Hegel–Marx tradition, but rather an end to all such theories. What we grasp through philosophy cannot be formulated in a theory; it is the insight into the multiplicity of language games whereby we see how they function and that each has its place.

The Wittgensteinian attack on epistemology as a foundational enterprise still leaves it open, of course, to any philosopher to pursue a special interest in the workings of language games in which special or primary use is made of such terms as 'knowledge', 'criteria', 'evidence', 'certainty' and so on. Nevertheless, one is constantly struck by resemblances between strands of Hegelian and Wittgensteinian argument. This is basically because they share a common adversary in the Cartesian tradition of epistemology; and what is more, they both dissolve the spell which it lays on us by placing the whole range of activities involved in making knowledge claims in the context of the larger life of the subject. Making and testing knowledge claims about objects is one among the many activities that we pursue; it is part of our form of life and only makes sense within it, and consequently can in no way provide the model for the whole. So argues Wittgenstein. Registering facts about objects itself presupposes an activity of the subject, a subject whose nature must be understood in different terms and the exploration of which, indeed, ultimately challenges the very distinction between ourselves and objects around us with which we started. So argues Hegel.

But the further tenor of their argument diverges radically. For Wittgenstein, the larger context, that is to say the life form, resists any theoretical articulation, and therefore any critical theory which might guide us in resolving its tensions and contradictions. For Hegel, the larger context is the activity of Spirit which, precisely, is essentially amenable to conceptual formulation. In its Marxist transposition, this activity becomes the praxis of the human social subject, which in turn must be capable of achieving, through its historical development, rational self-awareness.

Thus the tradition in which Habermas stands is not of immediate or easy access to philosophers of the English-speaking world; not only because there is less widespread agreement that epistemology must be dethroned, but also because where its claims *are* rejected or reduced, what seems to follow is that further systematic theorising is impossible. Epistemology gives way to what amounts to a doctrine of ineffability rather than to some more radical metacritique. To the Wittgensteinian, critical theorists may appear as just another band of fools rushing about over the ground which has just been so carefully cleared by the assembled reminders about the ways in which our language works; conversely, to critical theorists the Wittgensteinian may come across as preaching an obscurantist acceptance of the *status quo*. In this respect, the reaction to Wittgenstein can resemble that to Heidegger, with whom the later Wittgenstein has sometimes been compared.

Nevertheless, English-language philosophers can surely benefit greatly from the tradition of critical theory, and in particular from the work of Habermas; English-language social philosophy, theory of social science, and understanding of the epistemological ascendancy can all benefit greatly from an exchange with this school. This penetrating essay by Garbis Kortian, which places the work of Habermas in the tradition of metacritique, and indeed pushes it further forward in that tradition, is thus to be warmly welcomed. (It may be set alongside Thomas McCarthy's quite admirable, if more strictly expository, study, *The Critical Theory of Jürgen Habermas*, M.I.T. Press, Cambridge, Mass., and London, 1978.) There is in this relatively short introduction no place to mention the many strands and facets of this tradition which Dr Kortian distinguishes and relates. Our aim has been only to make the tradition itself more accessible by placing it in relation to some landmarks which are somewhat more familiar in the culture of the English-speaking world.

Alan Montefiore,
Balliol College, Oxford.

Charles Taylor,
All Souls College, Oxford.

Metacritique

Introduction

The intention of this essay is to reconstruct the philosophical argument of the Critical Theory of the Frankfurt School.

The Frankfurt School is the name which has come to refer to the tradition emanating from the *Institut für Sozialforschung* and its journal, the *Zeitschrift für Sozialforschung*, which, in the 1930s, embraced the work of Max Horkheimer, Theodor W. Adorno, Herbert Marcuse, Walter Benjamin and others. These names conjure up very varied writings and theoretical interests which do not necessarily coincide. It may even be questioned whether they have anything in common beyond the programme for a restatement of Marxism in the form of a 'critical theory of society' – a programme which found its expression in Horkheimer's famous article 'Traditional and Critical Theory' (1937). The very idea of a theory defined as critical theory seems scarcely compatible with the idea of a school and all that that term may connote: unity of thought and method, definition of orthodoxy, constitution of dogma, or even nomination of an official spokesman.

Is there only one Frankfurt School? This may be asked as an historical question, that is, in doxological terms. Even if this tradition were reconstituted in all its historical detail, however, the question would still remain as to whether the school was anything more than a literary circle. In other words, the question that must be asked is a philosophical one: what is the philosophical argument of Critical Theory? It is the philosophical question which will be pursued in this essay through reference to the work of Jürgen Habermas who is recognised as having given an original articulation to the heritage of Critical Theory.

In so far as the object of this essay is not to cite or summarise opinions, but to relate the fundamental thesis of the theory to its motivating presuppositions, the exposition of the philosophical argument can only consist in a *reconstruction*. The reconstruction of the argument will be accomplished through a return to the theoretical *locus classicus* from which the thesis of the Frankfurt School derives its meaning and its significance, and in relation to which its coherence may be examined and its logic demonstrated. This locus is Hegel's *Phenomenology of Spirit*. The more precise co-ordinates which define the Frankfurt School thesis are, on the one hand, the two fundamental concepts of the *Phenomenology of Spirit*, speculative experience and the speculative proposition, and, on the other, the fact that the dissolution of German Idealism threw these concepts into question. This double reference does not define only an historical location. The topology of the discourse is part of the argument itself. The Frankfurt School, through its relation to Marx, is founded on the experience of the dissolution of the Hegelian system. The Hegelian system which supports the twin concepts of speculative experience and the speculative proposition was precisely what Marx intended to invert. Thus, the point of Marx's dispute with Hegel is very specific. The inversion is determined by the paradigm of Hegelian thought. It is possible to distinguish the terminology of a theory from its paradigm, that is, the structure of argument which governs the articulation of the concepts in accordance with a logic which may continue to obligate someone who believes that he has freed himself from it through differences in vocabulary. It is not sufficient to invoke the celebrated 'epistemological break' in which Marx's theoretical enterprise is supposed to have originated, whatever the date of the 'break' may have been. This would be to forget that the epistemology which sustains the doctrine of the 'break' – a doctrine which is in reality a neo-Kantian survival – presents weighty philosophical problems. Philosophy must have the right not to be reduced to one of the theories of knowledge which have multiplied in geometrical progression since Hermann Cohen's call for a 'return to Kant'. Such a return to Kant is in danger of commencing by emptying the Kantian inquiry of its philosophical content. There is no reason to enter into the debate about the existence or non-existence of a break between Marx and Hegel at this or that date, so long as the presuppositions and implications of epistemology have not been clarified. This clarification requires an investigation at a completely different, and much more radical, level, namely, at the level of the presuppositions of a theory, whatever it may be. This is a question which relates to theory as such and which concerns every possible theoretical construction, whether theories of knowledge, critical or positivist, or whether theories which claim an absolute starting point such as classical ontologies or Husserlian phenomenology.

In order to open up this more radical level of questioning, it is necessary to deconstruct the structure through which the presuppositions which underlie everything that is advanced as positive theory are produced and represented. Positive concepts which take over words from ordinary language epitomise those presuppositions which, according to Hegel, are so 'well-known' precisely because they are not 'known'. The name Hegel gives to the totality of these presuppositions which always appear in the form of a cultural configuration (*Gestalt der Bildung*) is 'phenomenal knowledge' (*erscheinendes Wissen*). It is this knowledge which presents itself as the object of a *Phenomenology*. Phenomenology is defined as the science of an experience – the experience of consciousness or speculative experience. It is for this reason that the inquiry into the presuppositions of theory cannot avoid reference to the *Phenomenology of Spirit*, a text which aims to articulate speculative experience within the discourse of the speculative proposition. *Speculative* is to be understood here in its Hegelian sense as opposed to *positive*, that is, as opposed to that which may be defined by virtue of certain presuppositions which remain implicit. The elucidation of these presuppositions can only be accomplished through an experience which relates the positive to the presupposition which was the condition of its definition. This experience is the transgression of the limit between the positive and its condition. It is precisely by virtue of what is articulated through speculative experience that the discourse of the speculative proposition is to be distinguished from theoretical enterprises which are content to bring together different positive fields, and to pass from one to another by a transference (*metaphora*) which produces a synthesis in the metaphor and not in the concept.

What is metacritique? In what sense is 'critical theory', as it has so been defined since Horkheimer's article, a 'critique'? The word 'critique' must clearly be understood here in reference to Kant and to the status of the question of knowledge. Where then is the difference between the critical theory of the Frankfurt School and the numerous neo-Kantian restatements of the critical question which reduced it to epistemological terms? It is precisely at this point that the term 'metacritique' becomes necessary. The critique of knowledge may certainly extend its embrace to include other objects, as, for example, all cultural forms. Such breadth of vision in the writings of Ernst Cassirer could not make critique radical, however, as long as it failed to call into question the initial presupposition which sustains the critical enterprise as such. The *substance* subjected to the critique may change, the *function* of the critique remains the same. How can this presupposition which supports the critical enterprise be brought to light? A 'critique of critique' will not suffice. This would simply involve the contradictory demand that critique, ignorant of the dimension which makes critique possible, should make good its own defect. Hence metacritique. Thus Herder and Hamann, wishing to point out the blind spot of the critical question in Kant (the dimension of language), wrote, respectively, a *Metacritique of the Critique of*

Pure Reason, and a *Metacritique of the Purism of Reason.* In the same way, Adorno wrote his *Metacritique of Epistemology* to reveal the social relations which are always presupposed and never addressed by *prima philosophia* in general, and by Husserlian phenomenology in particular, which sought to rehabilitate first philosophy through the medium of epistemology.

In short, metacritique is true critique, or rather, it is what critique becomes when it is made radical. The critique of knowledge is limited by the fact that there is always something which it does not criticise. It does not criticise itself, in other words, its initial conception of what knowledge is. Knowledge, it is always assumed, must be subjected to criticism if we are not to be in danger of falling into error. This unquestioned conviction animates all epistemologies. In the Introduction to the *Phenomenology of Spirit*, Hegel showed that the critical question must be pushed to the point where the thesis advanced by epistemology is turned against itself: the 'fear of falling into error' may be in reality the 'fear of the truth'. Metacritique is to be understood here as this radical move for which Hegel's text provides the paradigm.

In the process of critique, the object criticized is subjected to examination, but the critical canon remains in the dark. There is no question of seeing the suspicion of error displaced from the object criticised onto the critical subject. The subject engaged in critique does not reflect on its relation to the object criticised. Were the critique itself to be subjected to critique and share the fate of the object criticised, then the 'familiarity' which sustains the critical enterprise would be revealed in its true strangeness. The discovery of the unknown at the heart of the well-known is the *experience* whereby what is known and trusted loses its familiarity, while the unknown which remained concealed is brought to light and becomes knowable. What is revealed here cannot be an ultimate foundation, posited in an absolute manner as in metaphysics. This experience reveals metacritique as a radicalisation of critique, and the movement associated with the 'meta' is only radical as long as it resolutely refuses any such absolute position.

Hegel, however, employs the radicalisation of critique, or this experience which he terms 'speculative', in the service of an absolute system of knowledge governed by the idealist presupposition of the identity of thought and being. The dissolution of the system led to this experience being almost completely forgotten and hence to the general diffusion of positivism in all its forms. The metacritique of positivism formed the basis of the Frankfurt School. The reference to Marx was aimed at the transformation of the Marxist critique into a metacritique of theory: the Hegelian paradigm was extended as the social relations concealed by idealism were made manifest.

The metacritique of epistemology is thus accomplished as critical theory of society. It exposes the presence in the Hegelian system of a positive element which had escaped the notice of that system in its claim to have uncovered all its conditions – socio-economic determination. This opaque core condemns the system to idealism. Metacritique, or recourse to the paradigm furnished by the Hegelian phenomenological experience, thus appears as the only way to avoid being caught in the snares of idealism at the very moment when it seems that one has finally escaped, whether by means of a 'break' between oneself and idealism, or simply by a sudden bout of amnesia.

The metacritical dimension of Critical Theory appears most distinctly in the work of Jürgen Habermas. His entire *oeuvre*, and especially *Knowledge and Human Interests*, may be regarded as an attempt to write a new *Phenomenology of Spirit* on a different foundation. In Hegel, phenomenological experience is used in the service of a knowledge which is the knowledge the absolute has of itself. In Habermas, the same experience culminates in a knowledge which cannot be absolute. It is the knowledge which man, a contingent being, has of himself and of the socio-historical conditions of his being.

I

The problem

In the Preface to *Knowledge and Human Interests*,[1] Habermas asserts that a radical critique of knowledge, that is, a metacritique of epistemology, is only possible as social theory.[2] The purpose of this essay is to discuss the implications and philosophical import of that claim.

Since epistemology came into its own in the course of the second half of the nineteenth century following the demise of systematic philosophy, it has sought to be understood either as a simple methodology of the sciences (as in neo-Kantianism), or as the elaboration of a universal foundation of knowledge to replace the ontology of traditional *prima philosophia* (as in Husserl's phenomenology), or as a simple positivism within the theoretical framework of the exact sciences (as in contemporary analytical philosophy).

The Frankfurt School is no less opposed to the recent attempt to revive ontology in the form of epistemology than to the scientistic epistemology of positivisms. The Frankfurt School defines itself as metacritique of all alike. The philosophical diapason of this metacritique is the concept of speculative experience and the theory of philosophical discourse which Hegel developed and exemplified in the

---

[1] Jürgen Habermas, *Erkenntnis und Interesse*, Suhrkamp, Frankfurt-on-Main, 1968, 2nd edn 1973; *Knowledge and Human Interests*, trans. Jeremy J. Shapiro, Heinemann, London, 1972.

Translator's note: references to French and German works are given to the original and to the English translation where such exists. In the interests of accuracy and uniformity, however, all quotations which appear in the text have been translated by the present translator.

[2] *Ibid.*, p. 9; trans. p. vii.

Phenomenology of Spirit. This runs through to the whole of Critical Theory from Horkheimer's[3] programmatic statement to the diverse writings of Theodor W. Adorno,[4] Herbert Marcuse[5] and Jürgen Habermas.[6]

A direct line of descent from the *Phenomenology of Spirit* to Critical Theory may be established because it was Hegel himself who first set out the metacritical argument as part of his explication of the concept of speculative experience. The argument was formulated as a radicalisation of the Kantian critique of knowledge and was to lead to the dissolution of all epistemology. In one way or another, the Kantian paradigm of *Erkenntniskritik* has been transmitted to all epistemologies, whether neo-Kantian in a strict sense, or whether appearing in the form of the contemporary structuralist variants. For this reason, Critical Theory is able to oppose the Hegelian paradigm of metacritique to scientistic and positivist epistemology and to attempts to revive ontology through epistemology.

The Hegelian concept of speculative experience and the discourse which it articulates is given a negative restatement. Critical Theory is intended as the experience and expression of the failure of the Hegelian concept. Yet, it refuses to become identified with any transgression of that

---

[3] M. Horkheimer. 'Traditionelle und kritische Theorie', in his *Kritische Theorie. Eine Dokumentation*, ed. A. Schmidt, Fischer, Frankfurt-on-Main, 1968, vol. II, pp. 137–91; 'Traditional and Critical Theory', in *Critical Theory: Selected Essays*, trans. M. J. O. O'Connell *et al.*, Herder and Herder, New York, 1972.

[4] M. Horkheimer, Th. W. Adorno, *Dialektik der Aufklärung*, Querido, Amsterdam, 1947; *Dialectic of Enlightenment*, trans J. Cumming, Allen Lane, London, 1973. Th. W. Adorno, *Zur Metakritik der Erkenntnistheorie, Studien über Husserl und die phänomenologischen Antinomien*, Kohlhammer, Stuttgart, 1956. By the same author, *Negative Dialektik*, Suhrkamp, Frankfurt-on-Main, 1966; *Negative Dialectics*, trans. E. B. Ashton, Routledge, London, 1973. *Aufsätze zur Gesellschaftstheorie und Methodologie*, Suhrkamp, Frankfurt-on-Main, 1970.

[5] H. Marcuse, *Kultur und Gesellschaft*, Suhrkamp, Frankfurt-on-Main, 1965. *Reason and Revolution – Hegel and the rise of social theory*, Beacon, Boston, 1941. *Hegels Ontologie und die Grundlegung einer Theorie der Geschichtlichkeit*, Vittorio Klostermann, Frankfurt-on-Main, 1932. *One-Dimensional Man*, Beacon, Boston, 1968.

[6] J. Habermas, *Theorie und Praxis*, Luchterhand, Neuwied-on-Rhine, 1963; *Theory and Practice*, trans. John Viertel, Beacon, Boston, 1973. 'Erkenntnis und Interesse', in *Technik und Wissenschaft als 'Ideologie'*, Suhrkamp, Frankfurt-on-Main, 1968. *Zur Logik der Sozialwissenschaften*, Suhrkamp, Frankfurt-on-Main, 1970.

concept which would simply be a form of indeterminate negation. This negative recasting, which nevertheless implies an appreciation of the metacritical purport, bears the stamp of the intervention of Marx. This intervention signifies an extension of the Hegelian concept of metacritique: the inquiry into knowledge is henceforth an inquiry into its genesis and social and economic application. Consequently, the status of Critical Theory differs from the status of positivism or philosophy as long as the latter remains identified with the question of self-foundation. The significance of Habermas's thesis which claims to recover the true import of the Kantian epistemological inquiry lies in this extension of the Hegelian concept of metacritique. In what follows, the stages in the development of this thesis by Critical Theory, and particularly by Habermas, will be examined.

2

Hegel and the speculative structure of Critical Theory

I THE METACRITICAL IMPORT OF HEGEL'S CONCEPT OF EXPERIENCE

The search to understand speculative experience which strives for absolute knowledge and knowledge of the absolute leads Hegel to embark in the Introduction to the *Phenomenology of Spirit*[1] on the metacritical dissolution of all epistemology, all critical interrogation of knowledge. The unmistakable butt of this attack is the Kantian concept of critique. The dissolution is brought about by the radicalisation of Kant's transcendental philosophy on the basis of the metaphysical presuppositions of Schelling's philosophy of identity.*

The argument on which Hegel's case turns derives its force from the following reflection: if, in accordance with the requirements of a transcendental philosophy, knowledge of an object is to be understood as the objectification produced by the synthetic activity of the subject, then the model pre-

---

* 'Philosophy of identity' refers here to the ontology of German Idealism. This amounts to a restatement for modern philosophy of consciousness of the ancient Parmenidean presupposition of the identity of thought and being. Kant postulates a 'transcendental affinity' or 'identity' between the subject and object of knowledge. The highest principle of all synthetic *a priori* judgements asserts the identity of the (subjective) conditions of the possibility of experience and the conditions of the possibility of the objects of experience. In the works of Schelling this principle is transformed through an interpretation of Spinozism into a system of philosophy of identity which posits the identity of subject and object, reality and ideality, nature and spirit, necessity and freedom. This identity reappears in Hegel in the form of a speculative understanding of life as concept (*Begriff*) or absolute spirit.

[1] G. W. F. Hegel, *Phänomenologie des Geistes*, Philosophische Bibliothek, F. Meiner, Hamburg, 1952; *Phenomenology of Spirit*, trans. A. V. Miller, Clarendon Press, Oxford, 1977.

supposed by the Kantian critique of knowledge cannot be maintained. The Kantian critique is based on the abstract reasoning of the understanding (*Verstand*) which, in its endeavour to be critical, separates the cognitive subject from its own objectified products, and from the process of objectification, in order to oppose subject and object abstractly. The result of this separation and opposition is that knowledge assumes the function either of an active *instrument* to 'seize hold of the truth',[2] or of a passive *medium* 'through which the light of truth reaches us'.[3] A semblance of justification for this procedure on the part of the critical understanding is found in its concern to secure the means of attaining true knowledge. Hegel's attempt to inscribe Kant's critical inquiry within his own system of reference, while it distorts Kant's own problematic, is nevertheless successful as a dialectical demonstration of the aporias in the epistemological model which he imputes to criticism. He shows the inconsistency of criticism with the essence of transcendentalism and reveals the unavowed presuppositions of its critique of knowledge.

For if knowledge is the instrument for seizing hold of absolute essence, then it is immediately apparent that the use of an instrument or tool does not leave the thing as it is for itself, but entails some transformation and change in it. If, on the other hand, knowledge is not an instrument in our employ, but a passive medium through which the light of truth reaches us, then we are still unable to attain truth as it is in itself but only as it is through and in this medium.[4]

In both cases, the desired immediacy results from the abstractions of the understanding. The critical ambitions of the understanding lead it to forget its essence as synthetic activity because it is confined to a representation of knowledge as an instrument or a medium, both of which are separated from the process, whereas knowledge is this process itself.

[2] *Ibid.*, p. 65; trans. p. 46.   [3] *Ibid.*, p. 66; trans. p. 46.
[4] *Ibid.*

The attempt to secure true and objective knowledge by eliminating all subjective intervention in knowledge (the effects of the instrument on the knowledge)[5] means simply that critique itself must surrender to the abstract reasoning of the understanding, which leads to contradiction and absurdity.

Where a thing has been shaped by an instrument and we then take away from it what the instrument has done to it, the thing – in this case, the absolute – remains exactly as it was before our wasted effort.... Or if, representing knowledge as a medium, we learn the law of its refraction, it is likewise of no avail to subtract the refraction from the result; for knowledge is not the refraction of the ray, but is the ray itself through which truth touches us, and if this were taken away, all that would have been indicated to us would have been pure direction or empty space.[6]

Moreover, the fear which motivates the critique of knowledge, 'the fear of falling into error',[7] betrays the same inconsistency which is at the heart of the whole enterprise: criticism neglects to direct its sceptical distrust towards its own assumptions and presuppositions which are regarded as established truths.

This fear does, of course, presuppose something, indeed, a great deal, as truth, and supports its reservations and arguments on what itself is in need of examination as to its truth. It presupposes representations of knowledge as an instrument and a medium, and presupposes a distinction between ourselves and this knowledge. Its prime presupposition, however, is that the absolute stands on one side and knowledge on the other, for itself and separated from the absolute, yet something real, or, in other terms, that knowledge, which being outside the absolute is presumably also outside the truth, is nevertheless true – a presumption which reveals 'fear of error' to be fear of the truth.[8]

Such an account of the Kantian concept of critique seems at first sight to be little more than a wicked caricature, especially since the negative conclusion at which Hegel arrives

---

[5] *Ibid.*   [6] *Ibid.*   [7] *Ibid.*
[8] *Ibid.*, pp. 66–7; trans. p. 47.

results from his own fundamental presupposition: 'that the absolute alone is true or that the true alone is absolute'.[9] When suddenly confronted with the demands of absolute knowledge, Kant's epistemological inquiry cannot avoid being dissolved within this system of knowledge. But, closer examination of Hegel's argumentation shows it to contain a metacritical moment which holds against all critical interrogation of knowledge, even though this metacritique is placed unilaterally in the service of absolute knowledge. The phenomenological speculative experience which Hegel propounds is indeed in a sense more radically critical than a simple critique of knowledge which resolves 'never to submit to the thoughts of others on authority, but to test everything oneself and only follow one's own conviction, or, even better, to produce everything oneself and regard only one's own act as the true'.[10] This is no more than a modern form of Cartesian scepticism. It is an expression of modern emancipated subjectivity as self-consciousness, an expression of the will of self-consciousness to find unconditional certitude in its knowledge. The critique remains abstract and leads to the nothingness of the indeterminate negation to which it gives rise. Consequently, it lacks the 'conscious insight' into the objectified products of mankind, into the structure of the system of presuppositions and preformations which Hegel calls the *phenomenal knowledge** of natural consciousness.

In contrast to the simple critique of knowledge, phenomenological speculative experience insists on a radical doubt, a 'self-perficient scepticism' (*ein sich vollbringender Skeptizismus*), which, in its *determinate negation*, takes as its unique object the system of the phenomenal knowledge of natural consciousness, and constitutes 'the conscious insight into the untruth of the phenomenal knowledge'.[11] This scepticism,

---

* This Hegelian concept is equivalent to that of positive knowledge. It covers both pre-scientific representations and cultural traditions as well as the strictly positive knowledge of the exact sciences. In so far as this positive knowledge appears as the 'well-known', the question of its phenomenal appearance, that is, its genesis, is not posed.

[9] *Ibid.*   [10] *Ibid.*, p. 69; trans. p. 49.
[11] *Ibid.*, p. 70; trans. p. 50.

understood in Fichtean terms as self-reflection or reflection on reflection, is 'directed towards the entire extent of phenomenal knowledge' and 'makes the spirit able to examine what is truth, in that it brings about despair with the so-called natural representations, thoughts and opinions which it is indifferent to call its own or alien'.[12] The task which the *Phenomenology of Spirit*, as the 'Science of the Experience of Consciousness', sets itself, is to decipher the process of genesis of this objectified knowledge in all its concrete configurations (which are those of the historical formation of the human subject) through the self-reflection of the concept.

The scepticism of the understanding ignores this knowledge in its abstract resolution to follow nothing but its own conviction. Thus it only secures unconditional certitude of its knowledge within a form of philosophical discourse which remains that of abstract argumentative reasoning. The nature of a philosophical discourse which is concerned uniquely with phenomenal knowledge must, according to Hegel, be determined in another way. This involves an immanent critique of the philosophical discourse produced by the abstract argumentative thought of the understanding.†

Hegel observes that in the case of the common judgements of the understanding the form of the proposition expresses a subject-predicate relation. This predicative relation is found inadequate for presenting speculative experience in so far as

† Hegel distinguishes the positive proposition of ordinary discourse from the philosophical or speculative proposition (cf. the Preface to the *Phenomenology of Spirit*). This distinction can be traced to that between *reflection* and *reflection on reflection* which Fichte first set out in his *Sittenlehre* (1798): 'The rational being is so disposed that when it thinks, it does not as a rule consider its thinking, but only what is thought, and loses itself, as the subject, in the object. But, in philosophy, everything turns on knowing the subject as such ... This can only come about if the simple reflection is made the object of a new reflection' (*Sittenlehre*, in *Werke*, ed. Medicus, vol. I, p. 425). The second reflection is not expressed in a judgement of the order $n + 1$ on a judgement of the order n. It does not belong to a metalanguage relating to an object language. It reproduces the movement of the genesis of the judgement, that is, the utterance of the proposition. A theory of utterance, if it is to be consistent, must proceed to this second reflection: see Vincent Descombes, *L'inconscient malgré lui*, Collection 'Critique', Minuit, Paris, 1977.

[12] *Ibid.*, pp. 70–1; trans. p. 50.

that experience *is a knowledge of what is already known in phenomenal knowledge, and hence a knowledge of knowledge*. In contrast
to the speculative thinking (*begreifendes Denken*) of philosophy
(Hegel's own), the predicative relation in the judgements of
argumentative reasoning is determined in an external way.
In its *negative* aspect, the subject of the judgement of the
understanding acts as 'the arbitrarily moving principle of the
content',[13] that is, the predicate. In this operation of predication, abstract reasoning is 'freedom from the content'.[14]

It is reflection in the empty ego, the vanity of its knowledge. This
vanity does not only express that this content is vain, but also that
this insight itself is vain; for this insight is the negative which fails
to discern the positive within itself. Since this reflection fails to gain
even its negativity as content, it is never in the matter, but always
beyond it.[15]

In short, it is the scepticism of the indeterminate negation
which gives rise to the empty nothingness of the ego. In its
positive aspect, the subject of the judgement is represented in
such a way that the content, as predicate, relates to it as an
accident. 'This subject constitutes the base to which the
content is attached and upon which the movement [of the
concept – G.K.] runs back and forth.'[16] In both cases, the
thought is incapable of becoming aware of the movement of
the concept which reflects on its otherness as phenomenal
object-knowledge. Speculative thinking is quite different.
Here, attention is directed at the concept as such and its own
movement. In speculative thinking, the negative moment of
reflection 'belongs to the content itself, and is the *positive*,
both as its *immanent* movement and determination, and as the
whole of this movement and determination'.[17] The negation
in this case is not an arbitrary negation of the ego which
by-passes all content in order to return to itself as an empty
nothingness. It is determinate negation, and by virtue of this
alone, has a positive content.

[13] *Ibid.*, p. 51; trans. p. 36.
[14] *Ibid.*   [15] *Ibid.*   [16] *Ibid.*   [17] *Ibid.*

It must also be emphasised that in the speculative proposition the representation of a fixed subject to which predicates relate arbitrarily is destroyed and the movement from one predicate to another is halted.

Since the concept is the true self of the object and presents itself as *its becoming*, the self is not a passive subject inertly supporting accidents, but is the concept which is self-moving and which takes its determinations back into itself. In this movement the passive subject breaks down. It enters into the differences and the content, and constitutes the determinacy, that is, the differentiated content and its movement, instead of remaining separate from the determinacy. The firm ground of the static subject occupied by abstract reasoning now begins to quake, and the object comes to be only this movement itself. The subject which fulfils its content ceases to go beyond it and cannot have other additional predicates or accidents. Conversely, the dispersion of the content is thus bound to the self; the content is not a universal which, if freed from the subject, could belong to several.[18]

The speculative proposition presents the self-movement of the concept and destroys the normal propositional form which is content to express the difference between subject and predicate. This difference seems to be obliterated in the speculative proposition: the subject is effectively passed over to the predicate and vice versa. If this is the case, then it would seem that the speculative proposition is no more than an analytic judgement in the Kantian sense, a tautology. However, it is only to the argumentative thought of the understanding that it appears thus. The identity of subject and predicate which is expressed in the speculative proposition overcomes the difference established by the ordinary judgement of the understanding. Nevertheless, this *Aufhebung* does not signify the destruction of the difference. The speculative proposition is understood as the adequate presentation of the identity and non-identity (difference) in the becoming of the concept (*im Werden des Begriffs*). Naturally, in accordance with the disposition of Hegelian metaphysics, this concept is understood as the absolute

[18] *Ibid.*, pp. 52–3; trans. p. 37.

mediation of subject and object, and it is by virtue of this alone that it becomes, in phenomenal knowledge, the object of the speculative experience of the *Phenomenology of Spirit*. This experience is produced by the *Aufhebung* of the difference between phenomenal knowledge and truth; this truth, which Hegel calls philosophical knowledge, is a self-reflective reconstruction of the first knowledge which is objectified as a result of the transcendental formation of the absolute concept, or, in other terms, as a result of the transcendental formation of the human subject. The perfected form of this knowledge of knowledge, the knowledge of the self of the metaphysical substance understood in modern ontology as subject, is precisely absolute knowledge.

2 THE METACRITICAL DISPOSITION OF CRITICAL THEORY

The problematic which will be sketched out in the following pages is in no way concerned to demonstrate the possible success of speculative experience and of philosophical discourse which would lead to absolute knowledge. On the very contrary. The historical fate of this concept and discourse has been the same as that of the philosophical system which supported them: both concept and discourse as such have been dissolved. Moreover, since Marx, who belongs with the history of this dissolution, the most valuable experience of post-Hegelian philosophy is the impossibility of such a speculative experience: philosophy is left to probe the implications of this impossibility. Philosophy is not simply required to renounce absolute knowledge, but more importantly for the practical dimension of philosophical theory, to denounce one of the constitutive moments of Hegelian speculative experience: the moment of recognition and appropriation (*Anerkennung und Aneignung*) of the phenomenalised totality of the absolute concept in its otherness. Philosophy must denounce the moment where the concept attempts to appropriate, just as it stands, an objective historical configuration of the social and political totality which Hegel termed objective spirit.[19] The Critical Theory of the Frankfurt School turned to the most radical origin of the dissolution of Hegel's system, to Marx. Thus the Frankfurt School is, in a certain sense, the expression of an acute consciousness of the impossibility of the concept of Hegelian experience as philosophy. It rejects the moment of recognition and appropriation because it is that moment, together with the presuppositions of Schelling's philosophy of identity and the immanent teleology of the absolute concept, which provides, in the practical context, the foundation for the well-known Hegelian reconciliations.[20] But, however much the Frankfurt School remained committed to denouncing the Hegelian system, its inquiry itself remained bound to Hegel's thought, in particular to the *Phenomenology of Spirit*, and above all to the paradigm of metacritical reflection.

In the first place, Hegel established that the rationalism of the understanding was unable, in spite of its transcendentalism, to exercise anything more than an abstract critical reflection. This abstract critique neglected to bring to light its own presuppositions (its phenomenal knowledge) and failed to elucidate its predeterminations because it did not recognise the only discourse capable of sustaining these configurations of consciousness, dialectical discourse. Critical Theory turns the Hegelian paradigm against the rationalist understanding and its empiricist counterpart as inherited by the various forms of contemporary positivist epistemology. At the same time, however, Critical Theory introduces social nature into the Hegelian phenomenal knowledge through reference to Marx. Horkheimer is thus

---

[19] This is particularly true of the concept of *Sittlichkeit* (objective morality/ethical life) in the *Philosophy of Right*.

[20] For detailed analyses, cf. K. Löwith, *Von Hegel zu Nietzsche*, Europa-Verlag, Zurich, 1941; *From Hegel to Nietzsche*, trans. David E. Green, Holt, Rinehart, New York, 1964. See also his article 'L'achèvement de la philosophie classique par Hegel et sa dissolution chez Marx et Kierkegaard', in *Recherches philosophiques*, 1934–5, pp. 232 ff.

able to insist on the importance of the social and economic determination of theory which accepts the paradigm of the abstract understanding, and which then builds upon it without ever perceiving in its phenomenal knowledge the aspect of *interest* which arises from the concrete historical configuration of social reality. The Hegelian metacritical paradigm forms the speculative foundation of Horkheimer's distinction between *traditional theory*, of Cartesian provenance, and *critical theory* which is associated with Marx. Critical Theory arises from Hegelian speculative experience and more immediately from the fact of its failure. Horkheimer follows Marx in interpreting this failure and this experience as an unfinished dialectic, that is, a negative dialectic which becomes for him the equivalent of materialism.[21] How this comes about remains to be seen.

In the second place, Hegel's metacritique demonstrated that the claims of Kantian epistemology to be free of presupposition was untenable when confronted with the existence of phenomenal knowledge. He therefore sought to rid philosophy of the problem of a beginning by recourse to the phenomenological point of view – at least in the *Phenomenology of Spirit*.[22] The Critical Theory of the Frankfurt School simply reproduces this metacritical paradigm in its merciless attacks on any rehabilitation of a *prima philosophia*. In his *Metacritique of Epistemology* and *Negative Dialectics*, Adorno maintains against Husserl and Heidegger that the epistemological research of the former which aims at the foundation of knowledge in transcendental subjectivity cannot do without an Hegelian concept of mediation and that its claim to be free from presupposition is consequently aporetic;

[21] Horkheimer, 'Zum Problem der Wahrheit', in *Kritische Theorie*, vol. I, pp. 228–76; trans. in *The Essential Frankfurt School Reader*, ed. A. Arato and E. Gebhardt, Urizen, New York, 1978, pp. 407–43. 'In materialism, the dialectic is not regarded as finished. Grasping the dominant state of affairs as conditioned and transient is not immediately equated with negating and overcoming it.'

[22] This problem is addressed explicitly in the *Science of Logic*. Cf. *Wissenschaft der Logik*, Meiner, Leipzig, vol. I, 1932, pp. 51–64. 'Womit muss der Anfang der Wissenschaft gemacht werden?'; *Science of Logic*, trans. A. V. Miller, Allen and Unwin, London, 1969, pp. 67–78.

similarly, Heidegger's fundamental ontology, which under-
took to replace Husserl's epistemology by positing the
famous hermeneutic circle of *Geworfenheit* and *Entwurf* in the
analysis of *Dasein*, seemed to Adorno to be a relapse into
Hegelian immediacy.[23]

Finally, Hegel directed his metacritique against the
abstract scepticism of the understanding. A philosophical
discourse, articulated by speculative thinking in the form of
the speculative proposition and acting as determinate negation, sought to elucidate the structure of the phenomenal
knowledge of natural consciousness and to transform this
experience of the false into a testimony to truth. Adorno
employs this same paradigm of self-reflection in all his
writings from the *Dialectic of Enlightenment* to the *Metacritique
of Epistemology* and *Negative Dialectics*, thereby establishing it
as a key concept in the philosophical discourse of Critical
Theory. As in Hegel, this concept is used by Adorno to give
direction to the immanent critique which is addressed to the
argumentative discourse of the understanding. It differs
from the Hegelian usage, however, in that it transgresses the
movement of the concept as found in Hegel. This transgression betrays the influence of Marx, elements of Judaism, and
Kant's practical philosophy. Adorno seeks in this way to
establish a theory whose status is such that it can only claim
truth through its own realisation in praxis. 'With the concept
of determinate negation Hegel emphasised an element which
distinguishes Enlightenment from positivist decadence ...
But when he made the known result of the whole process of
negation, the systematic and historical totality, into the
absolute, he transgressed the prohibition and himself fell

---

[23] Adorno, *Zur Metakritik der Erkenntnistheorie*, pp. 32 ff., and *Negative Dialektik*, pp.
47 ff.; trans. pp. 37 ff. Whether Adorno's criticism of Heidegger is justified is not a
question which will be pursued here. Heidegger's dissolution of epistemology also
follows the metacritical paradigm of Hegel's *Phenomenology of Spirit*. Cf. the discussion below, pp. 128–30. On the question of the hermeneutic circle, cf. Heidegger,
Sein und Zeit, Max Niemeyer Verlag, Tübingen, 1972, § 32; *Being and Time*, trans.
Macquarrie and Robinson, Blackwell, Oxford, 1967, pp. 188 ff., and H.-G.
Gadamer, *Wahrheit und Methode*, Mohr, Tübingen, 1960, p. 250; *Truth and Method*,
Sheed and Ward, London, 1975, p. 235.

victim to mythology.'[24] The transgression of the prohibition which Adorno imputes to Hegel refers to the prohibition of the Jewish religion on images of God or on speaking the name of God. The dialectic which Adorno conceives as determinate negation 'reveals every image as writing ... and teaches us to read in its every line the admission of its falsity – an admission which robs the image of its power and wins it for truth'.[25] This dialectic is unable to accept the reconciliation with the false consequent on the experience of the false. That, however, is precisely what the Hegelian speculative proposition contrives to do if its practical consequences are considered. Hegel never hesitates to transfigure the antagonistic structure of socio-political reality by recognising and appropriating the concrete objective configuration of the normative constraining otherness (*Sittlichkeit*) as the realisation and accomplishment of the supreme good. In Adorno's eyes dialectic is determinate negation and hence unfinished and negative: it can do no more than faithfully follow the prohibition on the image of God. 'The Jewish religion admits no word which would afford comfort to the despair of all that is mortal. Hope is bound solely to the prohibition on calling on the false as God, the finite as infinite, the lie as truth.'[26] Since this dialectic is unfinished, Adorno, like Horkheimer, calls it materialism. This means that the concept is not a self-sufficient movement, but is related to the historical and social context of material determinations which are conceived here only as constraints to be abolished. This demand for emancipation recalls what Hegel in the *Science of Logic* terms the 'presupposition of the unachieved end'. This, according to Hegel, lies behind the Kantian idea of duty (*Sollen*). Even if the end were achieved, subjectivity would know nothing of it because it presupposes

---

[24] Horkheimer, Adorno, *Dialektik der Aufklärung*, p. 37; trans. p. 24.

[25] *Ibid.*, p. 36; trans. p. 24.

[26] *Ibid.*, p. 36; trans. p. 23. This specific understanding of the figure of determinate negation as locus of truth plays an equally important role in Adorno's aesthetic theory: 'Keine Wahrheit der Kunstwerk ohne bestimmte Negation.' Cf. his *Aesthetische Theorie*, Suhrkamp, Frankfurt-on-Main, 1973, p. 195.

from the beginning that the good is something that eternally 'ought to be'.[27]

It is against this speculative background that Habermas defines the status of Critical Theory. Critical Theory propounds a normative concept of the emancipation of man through Enlightenment and a reconstructed philosophy of history which transforms Kant's philosophy of history via Hegel into that of Marx[28] in order to become a theory of evolution. It thus achieves a double reflexivity which reveals the retrospective and prospective disposition of the historical human subject. Critical Theory may therefore be defined in the following way:

The type of social theory which we first find developed by Marx is characterised by the fact that the theory is doubly reflexive. Historical materialism is intended to offer an explanation of social evolution which is so comprehensive that it extends to the conditions of the possibility of the rise of the theory itself as well as to the conditions of its application. The theory specifies the conditions under which self-reflection on the history of mankind has become objectively possible and it also specifies exactly who will be able with the help of the theory to gain enlightenment about themselves and about their potentially emancipatory role in the historical process. As a result of its reflection on the conditions of its own appearance and application, theory understands itself as a necessary catalytic moment within the very nexus of social life which it is analysing. Indeed, it analyses this as an integral nexus of constraints from the point of view of its potential *Aufhebung*. The theory thus covers a double relation between theory and praxis: on the one hand, it investigates the historical conditions for the constitution of a constellation of interests to which, as it were, the theory still belongs through its acts of cognition; and, on the other hand, it investigates the historical context of action which the theory can itself influence through the way it orients action. On the one hand,

---

[27] Hegel, *Wissenschaft der Logik*, Philosophische Bibliothek, Meiner, Leipzig, vol. II, 1934, p. 482; *Science of Logic*, p. 882: 'This repetition of the presupposition of the unachieved end after the actual achievement of the end arises when the *subjective disposition* of the objective concept is reproduced and made perennial.'

[28] Formally, and particularly when it exploits and revives the concept of Enlightenment, the philosophy of history which Habermas constructs follows the schema outlined by Kant in his 'Idee zu einer allgemeinen Geschichte in Weltbürgerlicher Absicht'; 'Idea for a Universal History from a Cosmopolitan Point of View', trans. L. W. Beck, in *Kant on History*, Liberal Arts, New York, 1963.

it is concerned with social praxis which, as social synthesis, makes knowledge possible; on the other hand, it is concerned with a political praxis which is consciously directed towards overturning the existing institutional system. Through its reflection on the conditions of the possibility of its own appearance, critique is to be distinguished both from science and from philosophy. The sciences ignore the constitution of their objects and understand their subject matter in an objectivistic way. Philosophy, conversely, is too ontologically sure of its origin as a first principle. Through its anticipation of the conditions of its possible application, critique is to be distinguished from what Horkheimer called traditional theory. It understands that its claim to validity can only be vindicated in successful processes of Enlightenment, and that means in the practical discourse of those concerned. Critical Theory renounces the contemplative claims of theories which are constructed in monologic form and sees, moreover, that all previous philosophy, in spite of the claims it has made for itself, has never had a purely contemplative character.[29]

[29] Habermas, *Theorie und Praxis*, Introduction, 3rd edn, Suhrkamp, Frankfurt-on-Main, 1971, p. 9; trans. pp. 1–2.

3

Habermas and Enlightenment

How does the question of metacritique fit into the theoretical space that has just been outlined? How does it follow from Hegel's *Phenomenology of Spirit*, or from the metacritical movement of speculative experience, especially in view of the intervention of Marx? Habermas's answer to these questions in his essay *Knowledge and Human Interests* is in keeping with the fundamental preoccupation of his critical theory.

In the first place, Habermas is concerned to rehabilitate the concept of Enlightenment by drawing the lessons from the classical critique of the aporias of Enlightenment provided by Horkheimer and Adorno.[1] The theory of Enlightenment turns on the categories of dogmatism, reason and decision.[2] These circumscribe the horizon within which the theory is developed. This horizon, as Habermas maintains, spans both Hegelian phenomenological experience and Freudian psychoanalysis. The theory of Enlightenment originates in an experience of emancipation from the constraints which arise when social and political relations are not transparent. In the controversy between critical reason and dogmatism, reason is not without bias. Reason, as dictated by the normative status of the theory of Enlightenment, expresses an *interest* on the part of the subject in emancipation at each stage of its critical reflection. The moment of decision, it must also be emphasised, far from being sep-

---

[1] Horkheimer, Adorno, *Dialektik der Aufklärung*.

[2] Habermas, *Theorie und Praxis*, 1st edn, Luchterhand, Neuwied-on-Rhine, pp. 231–57; trans. pp. 252–82.

arated from this reason, is in fact constitutive of it. The will which is resolutely committed to the reasonable is emancipatory in its moment of decision. The will releases reason from the constraints which have been imposed on it, it frees reason from the realm of heteronomy.[3]

Secondly, Habermas's critical theory follows Marx in posing the question of the legitimacy of the constellation *dogmatism, reason* and *decision*. This leads to the question of the justification of *critical theory* as such. This last question can only be answered through reflection on the context of social life which critical theory regards as a set of constraints to be overcome. Since this context is that of industrial and technological society, the characteristics of this society must be investigated.

Thirdly, Habermas is concerned to reinstate a concept of rationality inherited from the Enlightenment by carrying through an immanent critique of that scientistic-positivist rationality at the basis of the one-sided functionalisation of science in industrial society.

Indirectly, this critique is designed to prepare the ground for Habermas's metacritical project. It intends to provide a reconstruction of the way the positivist understanding works before proceeding to recover the experience of reflection which this understanding has forgotten.[4]

I DOGMATISM, REASON AND DECISION

Habermas starts to prepare the ground for the metacritical deployment of his critical theory by a discussion of d'Holbach, Fichte and Marx, the most typical representatives of what he terms 'decisive Enlightenment'.[5] The object of this discussion is to elucidate the relations between the concepts of dogmatism, reason and decision.

The concept of nature which is founded on the analytical.

---

[3] *Ibid.*, pp. 231 ff.; trans. pp. 253 ff.
[4] Habermas, *Erkenntnis und Interesse*, p. 9; trans. p. vii.
[5] Habermas, *Theorie und Praxis*, pp. 234 ff.; trans. pp. 256 ff.

and experimental sciences is, for d'Holbach, the embodiment of critical reason. Here nature is seen as a normative contrast to dogmatic superstition and prejudice. Positivist reason can appeal to its own analytical procedures to expose the blind mechanisms of a false consciousness objectified in the institutional norms of society. From the point of view of this reason, the massive objective force of prejudice has but one function – to consolidate the interests of an established power. The power of prejudice proceeds ineluctably from the ignorance of subjects who have no choice but to submit to the consequences: impediment to happiness, immaturity, reduction to slavery and heteronomy of action. Since the objective force of prejudice persists by laying fetters on the liberty and autonomy of subjects, the critical destruction of the untruth embodied in this objective force must appeal beyond analytical and theoretical reason to a cardinal virtue: courage, commitment to the reasonable. Critical reason can put an end to entrenched institutional dogmatism as soon as the will decides in favour of the reasonable, whose interest it believes it embodies.

Habermas, as always, sensible of the relations between theory and praxis, emphasises that the introduction of the moment of decision into d'Holbach's enlightened positivism and decisive reason makes it very different from contemporary positivism, especially in its relation to praxis. Since the postulate of *Wertfreiheit* received programmatic statement in the methodological essays of Max Weber, the human sciences of positivist allegiance have had to eliminate every practical aspect of theory in order to safeguard their neutral status as science. D'Holbach's enlightened positivism differs from its successors in a further respect: the identification of *truth* with *happiness* and *error* with *unhappiness*. To contemporary positivism this would simply be indicative of confusion between a cognitive category and an emotive category – a criticism which is indeed very plausible from the point of view of a reason which has been reduced to a single cognitive faculty. D'Holbach differs again from contemporary positivism in his emphasis on the resemblance between the laws of the physical world (nature) and the laws of the moral world. This resemblance derives from the equivocation in his concept of nature. Nowadays, it seems possible to brush aside this equivocation altogether with certain neo-Kantian premisses of Weber's methodology and Kelsen's philosophy of law. In spite of all the aporias this implies, the impossibility of drawing a normative judgement from a judgement of fact seems to be established beyond question.[6]

Following Kant's Copernican revolution in philosophy, the normative appeal to nature as a critique of dogmatism is no longer plausible. Nature no longer follows its own logic and regularities governed by causal necessity. When the transcendental subject became the Archimedean point of philosophy, the common epistemological presuppositions of the rationalist philosophy of the understanding and of the empiricism on which d'Holbach's positivism still depended were overturned. D'Holbach's *Système de la nature* would have to be replaced by a *System of the Synthetic Activities of a Subject* which henceforth prescribes laws to *nature* and norms to *freedom*. The presuppositions of transcendental idealism cause the concept of dogmatism to undergo a radical transformation. Fichte, the Jacobin philosopher of absolute freedom, was the first to draw these consequences. Dogmatism, according to Fichte, can no longer be confined to a set of prejudices and superstitions consciously imposed on subjects. It has universal significance and, in contrast to the pre-Kantian Enlightenment, encompasses the entire domain of nature, or, in Fichte's own terminology, the entire domain of the non-Ego. A consciousness which regards itself as determined by empirical nature, or subject to the influence of the non-Ego, is considered *a priori* as dogmatic. The principle of the dogmatic man is nothing more than a belief

[6] *Ibid.* Cf. Max Weber, *Gesammelte Aufsätze zur Wissenschaftslehre*, Mohr, Tübingen, 1922; Hans Kelsen, *Aufsätze zur Ideologiekritik*, Luchterhand, Neuwied-on-Rhine, 1964; Hans Kelsen, *Reine Rechtslehre*, F. Deuticke, Leipzig and Vienna, 1934; Ernst Topitsch, *Sozialphilosophie zwischen Ideologie und Wissenschaft*, Luchterhand, Neuwied-on-Rhine, 1962.

in the existence of things for their own ends independent of the Ego, or the indirect belief in his own scattered Self supported only by objects.[7] The concept of the scattered Self is central to Fichte's philosophy of consciousness. It constitutes the totality of blind mechanisms of the Ego in its otherness (the non-Ego) which escape the control of self-consciousness. In Fichte's words, 'the Ego is preserved in the scattered Self before its self-positing' (*das Ich ist in ihm vor seiner Selbstsetzung aufgehoben*). The scattered Self thus appears as an indirect ancestor of Freud's unconscious. Habermas, from his Marxian point of view, also sees in this the first sign of a reified consciousness, a false consciousness.

If critical reason, in this case, the Fichtean Ego, is to break down the barriers of rigidified consciousness, it cannot be satisfied with simple analysis and logical argumentation. Something much more fundamental is presupposed: *the interest of reason in emancipation*. It is this interest which above all else distinguishes the enlightened idealist from the dogmatist.[8] The difference between the two is solely a difference of interest. The Fichtean Ego is able to bring to light the hidden mechanisms of nature and rigidified consciousness only as a result of a motivation experienced as a need for emancipation. These mechanisms are illuminated through an original act of self-positing where the form of reflection is intellectual intuition. From the point of view of this philosophical reflection, Fichte's concept of reason can no longer be considered as a simple cognitive faculty separated from the will. The will, like Kant's faculty of desire (*Begehrungsvermögen*),[9] constitutes the essential element of reason. The will manifests itself in action (*Handlung*) which has a primacy over cognition and which makes the unity of

---

[7] Habermas, *Theorie und Praxis*, pp. 236–7; trans. pp. 259–60.; J. G. Fichte, *Erste Einleitung in die Wissenschaftslehre* in *Werke*, ed. Medicus, Leipzig, 1910–12 (Nachdruck, Darmstadt, 1962), vol. III, p. 17; *Science of Knowledge*, trans. Heath and Lachs, Meredith, New York, 1970, p. 15.

[8] Habermas, *Theorie und Praxis*, p. 237; trans. p. 260; Fichte, *Erste Einleitung*, pp. 17 ff.; trans. pp. 15 ff.

[9] Kant, *Kritik der Urteilskraft*, Introduction, Table of Higher Faculties; *Critique of Judgement*, trans. J. C. Meredith, Clarendon Press, Oxford, 1928.

reason possible. Fichte's idealism, by relying on these Kantian premisses, pushes the practical primacy of the spontaneity of the Ego to the point where all manifestations of the non-Ego, including nature, assume a reified form which the Ego is bound by duty (*Sollen*) to overcome through its infinite acts of original self-positing.

The limits to the Jacobin enthusiasm which enables Fichte to transform Kantian critique into absolute autonomy of the subject must clearly be found, if not in his own system, then at least in those of his successors, Schelling and Hegel, in the disqualification of nature and in the activism of the Ego. Hegel's phenomenological experience of consciousness demonstrates that the spontaneity of Fichte's resolute reason remains profoundly abstract. Indeed, Hegel considers that the decisionist activism and limitless spontaneity arise from a philosophy of the understanding whose two poles are positivist rationalism and moralising idealism. The indeterminate negation which proceeds from the abstractions of the understanding ignores the determinations arising from history and the objective ethical and political order of its time. This Hegel analyses as a symptom of the age. The phenomenological experience of a subjectivity emancipated by the 'abstract and negative power' of the understanding demonstrates to Hegel that the cultural world in which Enlightenment appears is not an harmonious whole at rest within itself, but is a torn and divided world. Enlightenment is the world of spirit become stranger to itself, an alienated world. The two forms in which this stage of consciousness is manifested, faith (*Glaube*) and pure insight (*reine Einsicht*), appear as inveterate adversaries, but they derive from a common source: incoherent and abstract subjectivity. Hence, the immediacy of faith secure in its belief, and the critical insight of enlightened understanding which attacks belief, are ultimately identical attitudes. The science of the experience of consciousness, the *Phenomenology of Spirit*, sees in the subjectivity common to both the result of a long process of spirit which is no longer able to recognise itself in its own objectified products, culture. Hence, diremption (*Entzweiung*), which is the *formative* principle of this age, initiates through the abstract reflection of the understanding a rigid opposition between the subjectivity and the objectivity of the ethical and political order (*Sittlichkeit*). This opposition can only be overcome through the recognition and appropriation in cathartic speculative experience of all the forms of objective determination of the historical subject. Such is Hegel's motivation in the *Phenomenology of Spirit*. Thus Enlightenment and the interest of reason share the fate of the subjective particularisms which derive their force from the negations and abstractions of the understanding.[10] However, the reflective experience which in this way translates the concept of Enlightenment into a form of self-Enlightenment also forms the basis for the many and famous reconciliations.

A third generation of decisive Enlightenment in the person of Marx now intervenes in this tradition in defence of the interest of reason. Marx refused to accept the consequences of the reconciliations in Hegel, or, more precisely, had experienced their historical failure, but he did retain two fundamental aspects of Hegelian philosophy. First, he argued that since Enlightenment manifests the interest of human reason, and criticises dogmatism in order to emancipate the human subject, it must therefore be understood as an *historical result* of the process of formation of mankind. Secondly, he maintained that this formation itself presupposes a process of social labour in the sense of a transformation of first nature.[11] This process makes emancipation from the constraints of first nature possible without thereby leading to emancipation from the alienating forms of social labour which are sustained by the massive constraining

---

[10] Hegel, *Phänomenologie des Geistes*, pp. 383–413; trans. pp. 328–55. On the aporias of Enlightenment as may be derived from the Hegelian model, cf. Horkheimer, Adorno, *Dialektik der Aufklärung*.

[11] On the presuppositions of the philosophical anthropology common to Hegel and Marx, cf. Manfred Riedel, *Theorie und Praxis im Denken Hegels*, Kohlhammer, Stuttgart, 1965, pp. 121 ff.

objective force of second nature, in the Hegelian sense, the institutional and ideological superstructures.

In this context, the concepts of dogmatism, reason and decision were to undergo a further radical transformation. The interest of reason in the emancipation of man can no longer assume the subjective form of a moralising self-determination as in Kant or Fichte. It must take on an objective, social form which is immanently free from the contradictions of a torn social world. In this torn world, superstitions, faith, institutional prejudices and the theories which are used to legitimise them serve an ideological function. They are manifestations of a false consciousness which conceal the interests of an established power. Consequently, the reason which combats them can only be a critique of ideology. This critique sustains a dialectical relation between *theoretical cognition* and *decision*. On the one hand, the dense mechanisms of ideology can only be illuminated to the extent that theoretical reason resolutely anticipates a social form emancipated from these predeterminations. On the other hand, the interest of reason demands a theoretically adequate insight into the process of the objective evolution of socio-economic relations, the only area where this interest can take on an objective form.[12] Thus, Habermas concludes, in the course of this historical stage where theoretical cognition reflects on itself in order to achieve a critical mediation between theory and praxis, Marx identifies reason and decision for the last time.[13]

2 THE JUSTIFICATION FOR A CRITICAL THEORY OF SOCIETY

Habermas argues that a certain idea of rationality derived from the theory of Enlightenment received its final statement from Marx, as did the great classical theories which reflected on the context of social life as a totality, sustained by the

---

[12] Habermas, *Theorie und Praxis*, p. 239; trans. p. 262.
[13] *Ibid.*

unity of an historical and social subject. Since the end of the nineteenth century, social and political theory has experienced great difficulty in reviving this idea of rationality which is regarded as outdated by analytic positivist rationality. This difficulty is explained partly by the overthrow of cultural and socio-economic relations consequent on the advent of technological, industrial society, and partly by the way in which the positivist sciences became seminal to the development of this society. The progressive disappearance of this idea of rationality has meant that the constellation of dogmatism, reason and decision has become extremely problematic, as has the relation between the theory of Enlightenment and praxis. As civilisation proves increasingly scientific and technological, so the mediation of theory within a social and political praxis as known to the reason of the Enlightenment seems increasingly constricted.[14] The laws which regulate the circle of production and consumption increasingly define society in terms of the domination of nature.[15] This domination brings with it a bureaucratic, rational and technological administration of other realms of social life. Within a system where science, technology, industry and bureaucracy are tightly interwoven, the theoretical power of a reason reduced to a simple cognitive faculty leaves no place for Enlightenment. The idea of the *emancipation* and *formation* of a socio-political subject through Enlightenment is replaced by the simple idea of *technical instruction*. The *socio-political praxis* of subjects in dialogue and communication with one another is replaced by *social technology*.[16] The analytic and experimental sciences which actively participate in the massive productivity of advanced industrial society have been able, as Max Weber anticipated, to transform the economic, social and cultural basis of human life radically, producing a similarly radical transformation in the deepest levels of the psychic structure of man. However,

[14] *Ibid.*, p. 232; trans. p. 254.
[15] *Ibid.*
[16] *Ibid.*, pp. 232–3; trans. pp. 254–5.

the one-sided functionalisation or instrumentalisation of
these sciences has impaired the critical force of the socio-
political theory based on the positive sciences. Critique is
nevertheless clearly indispensable both to theory in order to
clarify the social implications of science,[17] and to praxis in
order to raise the quality of human life. The question which
must be asked, and which is of central importance for
Critical Theory, is whether man in contemporary technological civilisation can avoid answering the essentially *practical*
problems (posed by praxis as understood here) to which
analytical and positivist sciences can only offer a technical
and instrumental solution dictated by the rationality of the
experimental and mathematical sciences.

If these questions have any meaning, then it lies precisely
in the opposition of *praxis* to *technology*, *action* to *technical control*,
and *Enlightenment* to *technical instruction*. It is not sufficient for a
socio-political theory or critical theory of society simply to
accept and reproduce the rationality of technological, industrial society by describing it in its own terms as a circle where
production responds to consumption. It must go beyond this
account and comprehend *society as such* apart from this circle
as being also an objective totality of interactions between
individuals who, through communication and dialogue,
become capable of autonomous action in socio-political
praxis. In so far as this social form does not exist, it must be
anticipated normatively, not as an abstract utopian possibility, but as a *real* possibility (*reale Möglichkeit*) in the
Hegelian sense of a determination (*Bestimmung*) or a concept
(*Begriff*) opposed to the existence of the object.[18]

The double reflexivity of such a theory, expressed in a
retrospective and prospective historical movement which
uncovers the conditions of its own appearance and anticipates the conditions of its application, also leads to a

---

[17] *Ibid*.; cf. also Habermas, *Technik und Wissenschaft als 'Ideologie'*, and H. Marcuse,
One-Dimensional Man.
[18] Cf. Hans Barth, *Wahrheit und Ideologie*, Suhrkamp, Frankfurt-on-Main, 1974,
pp. 61 ff.

diagnosis of the present age. Clearly, the diagnosis cannot
endorse the present social reality. It concludes that in
advanced industrial society the complex and close connections between production, scientific research, technology,
rational and bureaucratic administration and consumption
form the basis of our life and that we are bound to this in a
way which is both intimate and alienating. The present is
characterised by the paradox that the more the growth of
productivity and social development in our civilisation is
determined by specialised scientific and technological
research, the less this civilisation appears to be founded on
an adequate knowledge and consciousness on the part of the
subjects who form it. This disproportion sets limits to the
social engineering of the present.[19] It also presents contemporary man with a 'limit-situation'. A theory based on the
interest of reason in emancipation sets out to criticise this
disproportion by reconsidering the concept of rationality
upheld by scientistic positivism which, in the absence of
critical self-reflection, institutes in the name of Enlightenment the unilateral functionalisation of science and hence
relations of constraint.[20]

3 THE CRITIQUE OF THE POSITIVIST UNDERSTANDING

Habermas's metacritique proper begins with *Knowledge and
Human Interests* where a key concept of German Idealism is
invoked to delimit the rationality of the positivist understanding. This concept is 'self-reflection' (*Selbstreflexion*), or,
in Fichtean terminology, 'reflection on reflection' (*Reflexion
auf die Reflexion*). This, as we have seen, became Hegel's
'self-perficient scepticism'. Self-reflection may be understood as an instrument which makes the reconstruction of
knowledge possible. Hence, through self-reflection, the
transcendental formation of all objectified knowledge, all

---

[19] Habermas, *Theorie und Praxis*, pp. 231 ff.; trans. pp. 253 ff.
[20] *Ibid.*

objectification, can be understood, and the realisation of the science of the experience of consciousness in Fichte's *Wissenschaftslehre* and in Hegel's *Phenomenology of Spirit* is made possible. Stripped of its speculative pretensions to absolute knowledge, this concept of reflection upholds Habermas's entire metacritical edifice. The metacritique rests on the experience of reflection recovered by following the traces of its neglect in the scientistic thinking of the positivist understanding. Metacritique must therefore be preceded by a preliminary critique of the form of thought characteristic of this understanding, which can be defined quite simply as the neglect or rejection of the experience of reflection: '*Denial of reflection is positivism.*'[21] The neglect of reflection and the need for its recovery through critique is most evident in the premisses of the scientistic epistemology of the positivist understanding, and especially as expressed in methodological statements on the theoretical foundations of the social or human sciences. Hence the continuing interest of Critical Theory in methodological problems.

From a formal point of view, the Frankfurt School's metacritical programme may be best approached by a discussion of some salient points from its post-war polemic against the analytical and positivist theory of the human sciences. As we have seen, the essential objection of Critical Theory to the social and political theory of positivism concerned its constricted concept of rationality. For Critical Theory, this meant the loss of a concept of the unity of the socio-historical subject which could reflect on the social totality. It also entailed a separation of the decision inherent in the concept of reason from reason itself. The concept of the unity of the social subject was at the centre of the methodological controversy which led to a critique of decisionism and of the aporias of the positivist Enlightenment. Habermas's methodological debate with positivism, which follows in the steps of the controversy between Popper

---

[21] Habermas, *Erkenntnis und Interesse*, p. 9; trans. p. vii, 'Dass wir Reflexion verleugnen, ist der Positivismus.'

and Adorno, is informed by a critical reading of the historicist[22] and neo-Kantian tradition in the foundation of the human sciences and of contemporary philosophical hermeneutics.[23]

Habermas's essay 'The Analytical Theory of Science and Dialectics'[24] opens with the definition of the unity of the social subject as social totality which Adorno proposed in reply to Popper.[25]

The social totality does not lead a life of its own over and above that which is embraced by it and of which it is itself composed. It produces and reproduces itself through its individual moments.... Just as it is impossible for that totality of life to be separated from the cooperation and antagonism of its elements, so it is impossible for any element to be understood merely in terms of its functioning, without insight into the totality whose essence lies in the movement of the individual. System and particularity are reciprocal and can only be understood in their reciprocity.[26]

[22] Wilhelm Dilthey, *Einleitung in die Geisteswissenschaften*, in *Gesammelte Schriften*, vol. I, Vandenhöck and Ruprecht, Göttingen, 1959, and *Aufbau der geschichtlichen Welt in den Geisteswissenschaften*, in *Gesammelte Schiften*, vol. vii.

[23] Heinrich Rickert, *Die Grenzen der Naturwissenschaftlichen Begriffsbildung*, Mohr, Tübingen, 1929; Wilhelm Windelband, *Geschichte und Naturwissenschaft*, Frieburg, 1894; Ernst Cassirer, *Philosophie der symbolischen Formen*, Darmstadt, 1923, vol. I, Einleitung; *The Philosophy of Symbolic Forms*, trans. R. Manheim, Yale University Press, New Haven, 1955, pp. 73–114, and *Fünf Studien zur Logik der Kulturwissenschaften*, Darmstadt, 1961; *The Logic of the Humanities*, trans. C. S. Howe, Yale University Press, New Haven, 1960, On philosophical hermeneutics, cf. H. G. Gadamer, *Wahrheit und Methode*.

[24] Habermas, 'Analytische Wissenschaftstheorie und Dialektik – ein Nachtrag zur Kontroverse zwischen Popper und Adorno', first appeared in *Zeugnisse, Theodor W. Adorno zum sechzigsten Geburtstag*, Europäische Verlagsanstalt, Frankfurt-on-Main, 1963. On Critical Theory's methodological debate, cf. Adorno, *Aufsätze zur Gesellschaftstheorie und Methodologie*, Suhrkamp, Frankfurt-on-Main, 1970. Max Horkheimer, *Kritische Theorie. Eine Dokumentation*. Habermas, *Zur Logik der Sozialwissenschaften*, Suhrkamp, Frankfurt-on-Main, 1970. In what follows, I will rely almost exclusively on the article 'Analytische Wissenschaftstheorie und Dialektik' and the second part of the article 'Dogmatism, Reason and Decision' from *Theorie und Praxis*. I also take up here certain elements from my article 'Le problème de l'*Aufklärung* et de l'intérêt de la raison', in *Les études philosophiques*, 1973, 3, pp. 291–314.

[25] Habermas, 'Analytische Wissenschaftstheorie und Dialektik'; 'The Analytical Theory of Science and Dialectics', in *The Positivist Dispute in German Sociology*, trans. G. Adey and D. Frisby, Heinemann, London, 1976, pp. 131–62.

[26] Adorno, 'Zur Logik der Sozialwissenschaften', in *Kölner Zeitschrift für Soziologie und Sozialpsychologie*, 14, 1962, p. 251. Quoted by Habermas, 'Analytische Wissenschaftstheorie', p. 473; trans. p. 131.

Habermas insists that the strictly dialectical character of this concept of totality precludes any Gestalt theory or concept of totality which would be understood as something more than the sum of its parts, as criticised by the analytical tradition in the theory of science, in particular by Nagel.[27] Positivism may reject this category of totality as ideological or mythological,[28] but it nevertheless expresses a certain theoretical attitude: the subjects engaged in research in the social sciences study, in the name of scientific objectivity, a social context of which they are part, both in respect of their theoretical interests and their practical motivations. This thesis presupposes that society is a totality and that the individuals who objectify it are its subjects.[29] It therefore differs from its analytical counterpart, the concept of *functional system*, which is based on hypothetico-deductive premisses and empirical elements amenable to formalisation. The analytical concept of system thus denotes a framework of functional interdependence between variables, that is, empirical social facts. However, the application of this concept of system must be essentially contingent: there is no necessary adequation between the theoretical categories and the reality which is the social object. The model is borrowed from the physical and mathematical sciences. It is by definition 'abstract', that is, detached from the socio-historical context of the object and hence external to the object. The concept of functional system implies neutrality and indifference to its object. Such neutrality, sought in the name of scientific rigour and exactitude, in reality destroys the proper structure of the social object by perfecting rigor-

[27] E. Nagel, *The Structure of Science*, Routledge, London, 1961.
[28] Cf. K. Popper, *The Open Society and its Enemies*, Routledge, London, 1948, and *Conjectures and Refutations*, Routledge, London, 1963. Cf. also Ernst Topitsch, *Sozialphilosophie zwischen Ideologie und Wissenschaft*, and Hans Albert, 'Der Mythos der totalen Vernunft', in *Kölner Zeitschrift für Soziologie und Sozialpsychologie*, 16, Heft 2, pp. 225–55; 'The Myth of Total Reason', in *The Positivist Dispute in German Sociology*, pp. 163–97. For Habermas's reply, cf. his article 'Gegen einen positivistisch halbierten Rationalismus', in *Kölner Zeitschrift*, 16, Heft 4; 'A Positivistically Bisected Rationalism', in *The Positivist Dispute in German Sociology*, pp. 198–225.
[29] Habermas, 'Analytische Wissenschaftstheorie', p. 473; trans. p. 131.

ous scientific knowledge of one of its isolated aspects by the same method used to gain knowledge of an object of nature. Such a method condemns the theory to irrelevance. It precipitates the vengeance of its object, the social phenomenon: true and exact knowledge of an object of nature is trivial in a way which differs radically from the triviality of similar knowledge of a social object. The positivist analytical approach to a social object remains bound *nolens volens* to the constraints imposed by the social context of the object it is studying. Only reflection which understands the context of social life as a *totality* determining the process of theoretical scientific research itself is able to free the scientific approach of these constraints.[30]

In analytical theory, the problem of adequation between theory and object is resolved by a copy theory, a theory of isomorphism. Critical theory of society which presupposes dialectical, historicist, phenomenological and hermeneutic experience finds this unacceptable. The social object can never be understood on the basis of the empiricist and formalist epistemological presuppositions which are invoked as the conditions of the possibility of all theoretical construction. In so far as this object is the result of objectified action, it must, in conformity with the transcendental exigencies of critical theory, be *reconstructed*. Prior to all description, all analysis, and all scientific explanation, appeal must be made to a prior knowledge, or prior understanding at the level of the 'phenomenal knowledge' of the object, to use the Hegelian expression for what Dilthey was later to call *Verstehen* (understanding). The idea of prescientific understanding developed by Husserl and by Gadamer's explication of Heidegger's hermenuetic circle of *Geworfenheit* and *Entwurf* must therefore be recognised.[31] This, however, can only have an heuristic function for Critical Theory. Moreover, in order to avoid falling back on the primacy of an *a priori* dogmatic truth as would ensue from theoretical recognition of this

---

[30] *Ibid.*, pp. 474 ff.; trans. pp. 132 ff.
[31] Gadamer, *Wahrheit und Methode*, pp. 250 ff.; trans. pp. 235 ff.

Hegelian phenomenal knowledge, it is necessary to introduce the experience of critical reflection, thereby promoting emancipation from the dogmatic constraint inherent in this phenomenal knowledge. This brings about a fundamental change in the relation between *theory* and its *object* and between *theory* and *experience*.[32]

An analytical conception of the human sciences admits only one kind of experience. Only controlled physical observations which can be carried out by any researcher yield valuable results. A dialectical and critical theory of society, while it concedes a certain relative value and importance to empirical research, contests this constricted sense of experience. If there is to be an adequation, in the dialectical sense, between theory and its object, it is necessary to preserve the multitude of historical and cultural predeterminations of the social object in question. These predeterminations will never appear to an experience restricted to simple observation. Social theory is condemned to operate blindly with its concepts, models and constructions, following rules borrowed from an abstract methodology, as long as it continues to curtail its object by a restrictive concept of experience. Experience reduced to observation cannot take the place of reflection which recognises the predeterminations of the social object in a prescientific moment of understanding. This reflection opens up the way to a more profound experience of the object. It brings to light a complex structure of mechanisms invisible to simple observation.[33]

The amplitude of this concept of experience clearly connects it with speculative experience in the Hegelian sense, even though the relationship is a critical one. The extension of the concept of experience prepares the way for a consideration of the relation between Critical Theory and history. The Vienna Circle – in particular, Schlick, Carnap and Neurath – propounded a programme for the unity of science which

---

[32] Habermas, 'Analytische Wissenschaftstheorie', pp. 474 ff.; trans. pp. 132 ff.
[33] *Ibid.*

has continued to shape analytical social theories. They were able to defend this unity only by abolishing the temporal dimension completely. Time disappears in the methods of generalisation and formalisation which abstract totally from the difference between a social object and an object of nature. According to this theory, an historical event of the past must in principle obey the same laws as an event in the present or an object of nature. Even the prospective orientation represented by the predictions of the theory depends on empirical verification where the model of the present is inviolate. For Critical Theory, however, it is historical time which is determinative. Historical time creates a relation of *understanding* and an objectivity which does not operate in terms of constants and variables amenable to formalisation. As Rickert never tired of reiterating, an historical event possesses a uniqueness in the sense that it is irreversible, non-recurrent and non-repeatable. This certainly does not mean that it is bereft of objectivity. An historical event is universally accessible and may be determinative of a given epoch, thus explaining other phenomena. The universality of an historical law is that of a concrete universal in the Hegelian sense. It manifests the objective meaning (*Sinn*) of a social context of life. This justifies Critical Theory in assuming a *hermeneutic* attitude to the understanding of meaning. To understand meaning as a concrete universal does not mean to accept the forms of *objective spirit* dogmatically, but to take account of its *phenomenal knowledge*. The dogmatic moment of *understanding* in the act of hermeneutic interpretation must inevitably be placed in question by critical reflection if the theoretical subject is not to be lost in the manifold presuppositions of the object. By presupposing the neutrality of all theory, those who defend a simple analytical and descriptive method, and those who defend an hermeneutic and historicist method, risk falling victim to the immanent dogmatism of the object analysed. This explains the polemic against positivism and historicism, in spite of the importance accorded to the guiding idea in each: description and causal explanation (*Erklä-*

ren) in the analytic sciences and understanding (*Verstehen*) in the hermeneutic sciences.[34]

The critique of these methods is carried out by contrasting the *reality of the social object* with its *possibility*. This, as we have seen, is what Hegel diagnosed as a contradiction between the *determination* or the *concept* and the existence of the object. Adorno transformed this Hegelian idea, which had been employed by the Young Hegelians and by Marx in their critique of ideology,[35] into the imperative of Critical Theory:

> Theory must convert the concepts which it, as it were, brings with it from outside, into those which the object has of itself, into that which the object itself strives to be, and confront that with what the object is. It must dissolve the rigidity of the object as fixed here and now within a field charged with the tension between potentiality and actuality.[36]

There is, however, no immanent teleology presupposed in this Marxian dialectic to which Habermas refers as was the case in Hegel's. It is concerned solely with an attempt to understand society by retracing certain tendencies of its historical development and, in particular, by anticipating what the society is not yet, but what it contains as real possibility, in the Hegelian sense of the term, that is, an historical chance of realisation.[37]

At this level of methodological reflection, Critical Theory's relation to history betrays a specific understanding of Marx and refers back to a *praxis*. For an analytical theory of society, history is as 'inanimate' as nature: a model appropriate for the study of an object of nature is equally applicable to a social reality. The *practice* which issues from such a theory can only be a unilateral *technology*. The solution of social problems is hence envisaged in principle as a technical

---

[34] *Ibid.*

[35] Cf. Hans Barth, *Wahrheit und Ideologie*, p. 61.

[36] Adorno, 'Soziologie und Empirische Forschung', in *Sociologica*, ed. Horkheimer and Adorno, Europäische-Verlagsanstalt, Frankfurt-on-Main, 1962, p. 206; 'Sociology and Empirical Research', in *The Positivist Dispute in German Sociology*, p. 77. Quoted by Habermas, 'Analytische Wissenschaftstheorie', p. 481; trans. p. 139.

[37] Hegel, 'Die reale Möglichkeit', *Wissenschaft der Logik*, vol. II, pp. 175 ff.; trans. pp. 546 ff.

task. This confounds technical control with action, *praxis* in the broad sense of the term. The reflection which criticises society and the relation of the social object to history cannot admit such a confusion. It demands that social problems be approached on the basis of the uniqueness of the object, and that society be considered as an objective nexus of subjects engaged in actions, communication and dialogue.[38] This critique operates at the level of a philosophy of history in the retrospective and prospective manner made possible by the double reflexivity of the theory. It presupposes a radical experience analogous to that of Hegel and Marx, and therefore refuses to lose itself in the naïveté of the abstract rationalism characteristic of positivism whose fetishisation of isolated formalism tries to impose the imperative of neutrality on all scientific knowledge and all theory.

In this way, the Weberian postulate of *Wertfreiheit* is thrown into question. The origins of the postulate of *Wertfreiheit* are to be found in the neo-Kantian premises which set up a dualism between *is* and *ought* (*Sein und Sollen*). This was transformed in Max Weber's methodological essays, and later in the epistemology and political theory of logical positivism, into a dualism between *facts* and *values, scientific knowledge* and *norms, description* and *prescription*. From this strict separation of spheres there arose a negative methodological imperative: judgements of value must not be drawn from judgements of fact. Judgements of fact were understood as judgements based on an empirical description or on the hypothetico-deductive presuppositions which confer a logical status on empirical regularities. The result of this was that only judgements relating to the regularities of empirical facts could be true or false, while judgements arising from a normative sphere could be neither true nor false. These latter were nothing but 'empty forms' (*Leerfor-*

[38] Habermas, 'Analytische Wissenschaftstheorie', pp. 481 ff.; trans. 139 ff. Cf. Habermas, 'Theorie der Gesellschaft oder Sozialtechnologie? Eine Auseinandersetzung mit Niklas Luhmann', in his *Theorie der Gesellschaft oder Sozialtechnologie. Was leistet d. Systemforchung?*, Suhrkamp, Frankfurt-on-Main, 1971, pp. 142 ff.

meln), as Topitsch[39] calls them. In other words, they could never attain any scientific or theoretical status whatsoever.

For Critical Theory, the dualism which establishes a line of demarcation between *knowledge* and *value* in favour of scienticity is thoroughly problematic and far from being the great theoretical boon positivism pretends. This is indeed what Wittgenstein insinuated when he drew the consequences of the postulate underlying this dualism: 'We feel that even when all *possible* scientific questions have been answered, the problems of life remain completely untouched.'[40]

There has been no lack of philosophical attempts to provide interpretations of, and compensations for, the void created by the evacuation of the normative sphere and by the reduction of reason to scientistic rationality. Habermas, in the spirit of Adorno's *Dialectic of Enlightenment*, offers a brief outline of contemporary efforts in this direction. His account emphasises the way contemporary philosophy appears to Critical Theory as it casts an ironic glance at the spirit of the age of technological and industrial civilisation.[41]

The ethics of objective values in the phenomenological tradition (Scheler, Hartmann) transforms this domain into an ideal realm of being by investing values with an ontological dignity. These values are henceforth bearers of a material *a priori* and accessible only to intuitive knowledge. The subjectivist form of a philosophy of values is also unwilling to forgo an ahistorical sphere of norms and 'forces of faith' (Weber, Jaspers). Scientific knowledge is no longer complemented by intuitive knowledge but by a 'philosophical faith' which oscillates between pure decision and rational understanding. It finds itself compelled in practical social life to subscribe to one form or another of the competing spheres of values. This faith recognises the pluralism of these spheres without being able to resolve their dogmatic core. Finally, decisionism, in all its analytical, positivist,

[39] Ernst Topitsch, *Sozialphilosophie zwischen Ideologie und Wissenschaft*.
[40] Ludwig Wittgenstein, *Tractatus logico-philosophicus*, 6.52. Quoted by Habermas, 'Analytische Wissenschaftstheorie', p. 486; trans. p. 145.
[41] Habermas, *Theorie und Praxis*, pp. 241 ff.; trans. pp. 265 ff.

existential, anthropological, philosophical and political forms, does not hesitate to proclaim that all norms can be reduced to, and are founded in, the pure act of irrational decision. The fundamental value judgements posited as axioms by Richard Hare and the existential project of Jean-Paul Sartre arise from nothing more than simple decisions, or simple choice. Arnold Gehlen and Carl Schmitt offer variants based, respectively, on anthropology and power-politics. Man, for Gehlen, is 'the animal of not yet determined identity' and must commit himself in an act of choice to existing institutional norms, the instruments of his stabilisation. For Carl Schmitt, choice covers the selection of enemies. The invocation of mythology in the Heideggerian tradition (Walter Bröcker) is not surprising once the genuinely practical problems of man have been emptied of content by the positivist functionalisation of reason within technological society and once reason can no longer be recognised as the court of final appeal. Reason which has experienced an Hegelian dialectic of Enlightenment is quick to see the irony in the rise of this mythology. It complements the abstract positivist understanding as the mode of domination in our time.[42]

When faced with these compensatory philosophies, analytical and positivist theory has only one solution to offer – the take-over of all the practical and normative needs of man by its restricted concept of rationality. Theoretically, this amounts to a programmatic commitment to reason. This commitment sees itself as critical in its analyses of ideology and as enlightened. However, this theoretical position which seeks to uphold the postulate of *Wertfreiheit* stumbles once more against its aporias. A critique of ideologies which denounces all non-positivist forms of thought and action and which attempts to demystify all forms of life opposed to the progress of technological rationality can no longer vaunt the neutrality of its analysis. Its

---

[42] *Ibid.* The allusion to mythology refers to Adorno and Horkheimer's critique of Enlightenment in *Dialektik der Aufklärung*.

neutrality is compromised, first, because it implicitly assumes a normative concept of reason which makes it possible to conclude, for example, that behaviour based on the results of the theories of the empirical sciences and their associated technical instructions is rational because it is *efficient, economic,* etc. The concept of reason, espoused by the act of choice, is not, in this case, one value amongst others, but is a value with special status and may be the only way of realising other values. Secondly, the separation of *knowledge* and *decision, theory* and *norm,* which results from the postulate of *Wertfreiheit,* becomes problematic: the immense technological organisation of industrial society which is supported by positivist rationality has objectively attained such a degree of autonomy that it is able to dictate its own decisions and impose the reproduction of its own norms in all spheres of social life.[43]

Habermas concludes:

Technological domination over praxis, which is separated from theory by that fact alone, lends an oppressively apposite significance to Schelling's romantic definition of reason as regulated madness. If that central motive of reason which shaped myth, religion and philosophy now lives on in a perverted way in madness – namely, to bring the manifold of formless appearances into the unity and coherence of a world – then the sciences which snatch empirical isomorphisms from contingency in an essentially 'worldless' flood of appearances are positivistically purified of madness. The sciences regulate, but it is no longer madness that they regulate. Madness must therefore go unregulated. Reason would only prevail were it in both at once. As it is, reason falls between both. The danger of an exclusively technological civilisation which dispenses with the connections between theory and praxis can thus be clearly grasped: it is threatened by the splitting of consciousness and by the splitting of men into two classes – the social engineers and the inmates of closed institutions.[44]

[43] *Ibid.,* p. 246; trans. p. 270.
[44] *Ibid.,* pp. 256–7; trans. pp. 281–2

4

Knowledge and interest

Restricted rationality and the positivist epistemology which promotes it are testimony to the neglect of the experience of reflection. This rationality brings about the unilateral functionalisation of scientific knowledge in advanced industrial society. It reproduces at a conceptual level the structure and presuppositions of the established socio-political order. If this is so, argues Habermas, who is always alive to the liberating intention of Enlightenment, then the effective deployment of critical reflection must release an emancipatory force fired by the interest of reason. It is possible to lead the subject to an awareness of its reflective operations by relying on its interest in knowledge for the sake of knowledge and by presenting it with the opportunity to become transparent to itself through the reconstruction of the genesis of its own determinations. At the same time, this reconstruction restores a concept of rationality which does justice to its Kantian origins and its deployment in German Idealism. 'In self-reflection, knowledge for the sake of knowledge comes to coincide with the interest in autonomy; for the act of reflection knows itself as a movement of emancipation. Reason is simultaneously subject to the interest in reason. Reason, it can be said, pursues an emancipatory cognitive interest which aspires to the act of reflection as such.'[1]

Habermas proposes to realise his programme for the metacritique of epistemology on the basis of this theoretical and *normative* presupposition, while still following the model

[1] Habermas, *Erkenntnis und Interesse*, p. 244; trans. pp. 197–8.

of the *Phenomenology of Spirit*. Thus he turns once more to that fundamental conceptual instrument of Hegelian speculative experience and of the philosophical discourse in which it is inscribed, the concept of *self-reflection*. This renewal of Hegel's phenomenological project is careful to purge speculative experience of the absolute concept and of absolute knowledge. It is replaced by the experience of a reflection which illuminates the relation between knowledge and interest in a contingent being, man, amidst socio-historical conditions and determinations which are in turn contingent.

In the following account, I will examine first how Habermas presents the relation between theoretical knowledge and the interest of reason by placing it in the context of the Kantian and Fichtean thesis of the primacy of action. The act of emancipatory self-reflection reveals the interest which has motivated and directed all knowledge.

Secondly, I will show how Habermas understands the sense in which Hegel's phenomenology constitutes a radicalisation of transcendental philosophy. By emphasising the metacritical moment in the *Phenomenology of Spirit*, it is possible to understand knowledge within the context of the process of formation of the human subject. In this way, it is also possible to counter the aporias in Hegel's thought by introducing a reflection which (a) reasserts the relevance of Kant's epistemological inquiry dissolved by Hegel in favour of absolute knowledge, (b) exploits the way in which Marx extended the range of the Hegelian concept of metacritique, and (c) pays close attention to the way the onto-theological constitution of Hegelian metacritique is transformed into an anthropology. This anthropology is founded on an interpretation of Marx and of certain categories from Hegel's *Jena Philosophy of Spirit*.[2]

The argument here takes the following form: the radi-

[2] Habermas, 'Arbeit und Interaktion, Bemerkungen zu Hegels Jenenser "Philosophie des Geistes"', in *Technik und Wissenschaft als 'Ideologie'*, pp. 9–47; 'Labor and Interaction: Remarks on Hegel's Jena *Philosophy of Mind*', in *Theory and Practice*, pp. 142–69. *Erkenntnis und Interesse*, pp. 36–87; trans. pp. 25–64.

calisation of Kant's transcendentalism and epistemological inquiry leads to the dissolution of epistemology in the *Phenomenology of Spirit*. This follows from the goal which Hegel proposes: to attain the absolute knowledge potentially present from the very first page of the Introduction. This, in turn, follows from the presuppositions taken over from Schelling's philosophy of identity. However, the radicalisation brought about by 'self-perficient scepticism' or self-reflection is found to betray the same unacknowledged presuppositions as Kantian epistemology. Its own aporias come to light as it develops the dialectic of the phenomenal knowledge of natural consciousness. This consciousness must be recognised and overcome at each stage of speculative experience. Moreover, while Hegel's ever-present dialectic of the 'false' leads the way to truth by reconstructing the various stages in the formative process of the human subject, the omnipresence of an essentially ethical category (*Sittlichkeit*) threatens to absorb a quite distinct anthropological dimension which is equally constitutive and equally original: the behaviour of man in relation to nature. This concerns a material praxis, *labour*, which is expressed in *instrumental action*. This explains and justifies the critical appeal to Marx against Hegel, not only as far as absolute knowledge is concerned, but more particularly, in relation to the sublimation of the concept of labour in the teleological dialectical movement of absolute objective morality (*absolute Sittlichkeit*) which the *Phenomenology* presupposes. The reappraisal of the concept of labour enables Marx to reconstruct and decipher, this time in a critical way, the process of the formation of humanity on the basis of the laws of social and economic production and reproduction. Nevertheless, this investigation also runs a risk, which Habermas clearly identifies. It reduces the entire sphere of *social interaction* to the single paradigm of *material praxis*, that is, *social production* or *instrumental action*. *Social interaction* (Hegel) and *social production* (Marx) appear to Habermas as two *irreducible* paradigms. The two spheres which these paradigms regulate and constitute must be distinguished. These are, namely, the domain of the *human* or *hermeneutic sciences* (interaction and communication through linguistic symbols) and the domain of the *exact* or *nomological sciences* (labour, instrumental action). The reconstruction of these two anthropological domains fundamental to the process of formation of the human subject can be achieved through a self-reflection on the part of these sciences, and can thus lead to a reconsideration of the significance of Kant's epistemological inquiry as a critique of knowledge which, in this radicalised form, is only possible as social theory.

Finally, I will examine the problem of the self-reflection of science. Here the decisive influence is that of Hegelian phenomenological reflection. Certainly, Habermas does not take the phenomenal knowledge of an Hegelian natural consciousness as the starting point for this self-reflection. He does, however, refer to the *phenomenalised scientific knowledge* which appears in the positive forms of the exact sciences of nature, the physico-mathematical sciences, the socio-historical sciences and the human sciences. The historicist presuppositions of Dilthey, Rickert and Cassirer are adduced to sanction the distinction between the natural and human sciences. Charles S. Peirce's systematic inquiry into the logic of scientific research and Wilhelm Dilthey's account of the foundation of the human sciences are found to contain the germs of a self-reflection of science which would reveal the connections between knowledge and the objective context of social life. These two authors did not achieve this self-reflection, but, in the course of their methodological investigations, they stumbled on the interest which guides scientific knowledge. Moreover, their methodological reflection enabled them to go beyond the simple positivism characteristic of Comte or Mach. Positivism, in spite of its continuing influence, has increasingly lost the Kantian understanding of epistemology. Like certain contemporary analytical philosophers, it reduces epistemology to a simple theory of science dictated by the model of the physical and mathematical sciences. This theory of science represents the neglect of reflection *par excellence*. The contemporary renewal of this neglect consequently justifies the reconstruction of positivism undertaken in *Knowledge and Human Interests*.[3]

I THE PRIMACY OF PRACTICAL REASON IN KANT AND FICHTE

The problem of the interest of reason appears in Kant's *Grundlegung zur Metaphysik der Sitten* in the form of the question as to how pure reason can become practical. After discussing the paradoxes attendant on posing the problem in this way, Habermas directs his attention to Kant's attempt to transpose the concept of the interest of reason into all the faculties of the mind. In this way Kant is able to extend the normative significance of the interest of reason in emancipation by investing it with a cognitive import. He is thus led to uncover an interested motivation in knowledge itself. The transposition of the concept of the interest of reason into all the faculties of the mind is carried out in the *Critique of Practical Reason*. This Kantian project later incited Habermas himself to attempt a differentiation of the concept of the interest of reason and to subordinate the two anthropological categories mentioned earlier to two forms of interest. Instrumental action becomes subsumed under an *instrumental and technical cognitive interest*, and social interaction becomes subsumed under a *practical cognitive interest*. Finally, critical theory corresponds to an emancipatory cognitive interest: we will return to this later.[4]

In the third chapter of the Dialectic of Pure Practical Reason in the *Critique of Practical Reason*, Kant attributes an interest to each faculty of the mind,[5] 'that is, a principle

[3] Habermas, *Erkenntnis und Interesse*, p. 9; trans. p. vii.

[4] Habermas, *Erkenntnis und Interesse*, 2nd edn, pp. 367–417. This differentiation of the concept of interest has also been suggested by K. O. Apel, 'Wissenschaft als Emanzipation? eine kritische Würdigung der Wissenschaftskonzeption der *Kritischen Theorie*', in *Transformation der Philosophie*, Suhrkamp, Frankfurt-on-Main, 1973, vol. II, pp. 128 ff.

[5] Kant, *Kritik der Praktischen Vernunft*, Philosophische Bibliothek, Meiner, Hamburg, 1952, p. 138; *Critique of Practical Reason*, trans. L. W. Beck, Liberal Arts, New York, 1956, p. 124.

which contains the condition under which alone the exercise of the faculty is furthered'.

Reason, as the faculty of principles, determines the interest of all powers of mind, but its own interest it determines itself. The interest of its speculative use consists in the cognition of the object up to the highest *a priori* principles. The interest of its practical use consists in the determination of the will with respect to the final and perfect end.[6]

Throughout this entire chapter, Kant's argumentation is concerned to subordinate speculative or theoretical interest to practical interest, and consequently, theoretical to practical reason. 'To be subordinated to speculative reason and thus to invert the order, can in no way be expected of pure practical reason, because all interest is ultimately practical, and even the interest of speculative reason is only conditioned and complete in practical use alone.'[7] Kant's interest of reason which was developed out of the concept of practical reason therefore ends up submitting to that same practical reason. This allows Habermas not only to see in this a legitimate use of theoretical reason for practical ends, but to attribute to practical reason the role of an interest which is able to motivate and direct all theoretical cognition. Nevertheless, Habermas recognises a certain ambivalence in the Kantian argument in relation to the interested use of speculative reason, that is, theoretical reason. This ambivalence arises from Kant's equivocation with regard to the unity of theoretical and practical reason. This was a reproach which German Idealism never tired of repeating and which Habermas takes up for the same reasons but with a different end in view: to draw the most radical consequences from the concept of the primacy of action which supports the entire edifice of transcendental philosophy.

Fichte, whose philosophy presupposes Kant's practical reason and hence the primacy of action as the presupposition of all theory, put an end to this Kantian equivocation. Fichte took the step of establishing the dependence of theoretical

[6] *Ibid.*   [7] *Ibid.*

reason on practical reason. By conceiving of intellectual intuition as a reflected action, Fichte transforms the primacy of practical reason, and hence the dependence of theoretical reason on practical reason, into a *principle*.[8] This radicalisation of Kant is tantamount to founding the unity of theoretical reason and practical reason of the primacy of the latter. This provides Habermas with the theoretical framework he requires in order to determine the relations between *action*, *knowledge*, *the interest of reason* and *emancipation*. Habermas, who understands the Fichtean act of self-reflection as extending the Kantian concept of critique, is now able to define critique as the unity of knowledge and interest. The act of self-reflection thus ordains the status of philosophical discourse. In a prospective moment, this act is understood as normative, and appears as motivated by an interest of reason in emancipation. In a retrospective and reconstructive moment, this reflection is required to reveal the interested character of all theoretical knowledge, hence presupposing the primacy of action. This concept of action therefore embraces both an ethical and social dimension and an anthropological and epistemological dimension. The primacy of the *practical* is expressed in the form of a thesis implicit in all Habermas's theoretical works: action is the presupposition of knowledge, wanting-to-act is the presupposition of being-able-to-know. This thesis calls to mind the Kantian idea that 'reason only understands what it itself produces according to its own plan'.[9] This idea was taken up by German Idealism and traces of it may still be found in Nietzsche. The Nietzschean version runs: 'We are only able to understand what we are able to *do* – *if*, indeed, there is any such thing as understanding.'[10] The central category of German Idealism, action, is thus exploited in all its richness for metacritical ends. The unity of theory and praxis, *perceptio* and *appetitus* (Leibniz), *Vorstellung* and *Herstellung* (Heidegger), as well as the

---

[8] Habermas, *Erkenntnis und Interesse*, pp. 253 ff.; trans. 205 ff.

[9] Kant, *Kritik der Reinen Vernunft*, 2. Vorrede; *Critique of Pure Reason*, trans. Kemp Smith, Macmillan, London, 1929, Preface to Second Edition.

[10] F. Nietzsche, *Morgenröte*, Zweites Buch § 125, Taschenausgabe, p. 126.

possibility and goal of all theoretical knowledge, are reduced to the primacy of action and an interested praxis. Clearly these unities are intimately connected with the will to power which most eminently characterises the ontology of modern subjectivity.[11] The interest inherent in all theoretical activity is thus made manifest. Metaphysical considerations apart, interest for Habermas 'refers primarily to anthropological determinations. It enables him to denounce the highly problematic character of all pretensions to theoretical neutrality, whether in the pure contemplative theory of philosophy or in scientific theory. The Frankfurt School's critique of first philosophy or ontology and of the ideology of *Wertfreiheit* is to be understood in this context.[12]

In a wider perspective, the conclusions of Critical Theory confirm Nietzsche's diagnosis of the pretended neutrality of science. An aphorism from *The Gay Science* entitled 'How we too are pious' elegantly recalls the extent to which scientific knowledge is interested notwithstanding the neutrality it parades and the rigour and discipline of its self-imposed regime which leads it to abandon all conviction in the name of truth. Nietzsche claims that this interest has been concealed behind a metaphysical faith since Plato: 'It is still a metaphysical faith on which our faith in science rests – we, godless, antimetaphysical seekers after knowledge still light our torch at the fire kindled by a faith thousands of years old, the faith of Christians which was the faith of Plato, that God is truth and that truth is divine.'[13] But Nietzsche, as Habermas shows, saw in these convictions only symp-

---

[11] Cf. M. Heidegger, 'Die Zeit des Weltbildes', in *Holzwege*, Klostermann, Frankfurt-on-Main, 1950, pp. 69–104; 'Nietzsches Wort "Gott ist tot"', *ibid.*, pp. 193–247. Also his *Nietzsche*, Neske, Pfullingen, 1961, vols. I and II. Cf. Manfred Riedel, *Theorie und Praxis im Denken Hegels*, especially chapter 7, 'Hegel und das Herrschaftsdenken der europäischen Metaphysik', pp. 164–78.

[12] Cf. especially Habermas's inaugural lecture at the University of Frankfurt, 'Erkenntnis und Interesse', published in *Technik und Wissenschaft als 'Ideologie'*, pp. 146–68; *Knowledge and Human Interests*, Appendix, pp. 301–17.

[13] F. Nietzsche, *Die fröhliche Wissenschaft*; *The Gay Science*, trans. Walter Kaufmann, Vintage Books, New York, 1974, aphorism 334. H. Birault offers a brilliant Heideggerian interpretation of this aphorism in the *Revue de métaphysique et de morale*, 1962, pp. 25–64.

toms and used his insight only negatively to cast doubt on science.[14]

Rational knowledge itself refers to the praxis which presided over its genesis and to its direct or indirect application; therefore, once the interested character of rational knowledge has been revealed, whether in an affirmative form as in Kant and Fichte or in the negative form Habermas upbraids in Nietzsche, the metacritical elucidation of the relation between interest and knowledge follows the double movement of the concept of self-reflection.

In its retrospective moment, critical reflection reveals this interest by questioning the relation between the fundamental forms of knowledge objectified in the natural and hermeneutic sciences and the context of social life. It counters the aporias of an epistemological inquiry which abstracts from the objective context of the genesis of all knowledge and all theory (cf. chapter 4 section 2). It defends the relevance of a theory of knowledge which places the 'problem of knowledge' within the process of formation of the historical human subject (cf. chapter 4 sections 3, 4, 5).

In its prospective and normative moment, this reflection unites critique with the emancipatory cognitive interest by adumbrating the objective conditions of the context of application of the theory. This leads Habermas to elaborate a theory of communication centred on the concept of a universal pragmatics. This concept is explicated through discussion of Chomsky's generative grammar and Searle's speech-act theory. The task of universal pragmatics is to set out the necessary and sufficient conditions of a possible communication which operates counterfactually,* to diagnose the splitting of symbols produced in speech subjected to systematic distortions, and to attempt in this way to create the regulative canons of a constraint-free communication

---

* 'Counterfactual' describes the norm in relation to the facts which it is to measure. To speak of 'distorted' communication implies a reference to the ideal of a successful communication. The function of such an ideal is critical or 'counterfactual'.

[14] Habermas, *Erkenntnis und Interesse*, pp. 332–64; trans. pp. 274–300.

which has recognised normative force. The regulative aspect of universal pragmatics is related in turn to the model of psychoanalytic therapy: *Knowledge and Human Interests* treats Freudian metapsychology as a scientific form of self-reflection (cf. chapter 5 section 1).

2 KANTIAN CRITIQUE AND HEGELIAN METACRITIQUE

Since the time of Kant epistemology has been in crisis. The task of metacritique in relation to this crisis is to elucidate the relation between knowledge and interest. Habermas's perception of the impasse facing epistemology can be expressed thus: Kant's critical concept of rationality has either been usurped by Hegel's absolute knowledge or liquidated by positivist scientism. As a result, an objective configuration as important as the phenomenon of science has not been addressed philosophically in its full extent and significance since Kant. From the point of view of the exigencies of Hegelian absolute knowledge, scientific knowledge could only appear as a restricted form of knowledge whose limits were to be transcended. On the other hand, when the model of scientific knowledge becomes exclusive, as in positivism, the progressive reduction of knowledge and epistemology to a simple theory of science, to a simple methodological description, is inevitable. This reduction is part of a total capitulation before science which results in the philosophical import of epistemology being replaced by simple methodological description.[15]

In this context, it is not enough for theory to propose a simple and abstract return to Kant's critique of knowledge. The recovery of the original import of this critique must be accompanied by a metacritical radicalisation of Kant's transcendentalism. This entails continuing the process already started in Hegel's *Phenomenology of Spirit* of retrieving the experience of reflection which criticism could not redact and the neglect of which is positivism. The Hegelian metacritique, however, was executed on the basis of the presuppositions of

[15] *Ibid.*, pp. 11 ff.; trans. pp. 3 ff.

Schelling's philosophy of identity which compelled it to seek absolute knowledge. Metacritique thus became caught up in new aporias which must be resolved in turn.

The point that arrests Habermas's attention in the Hegelian metacritique is its treatment of epistemology's claim to be free from presupposition. Hegel's elucidation of this claim presents Habermas with the means whereby he can appropriate the fundamental argument of the *Phenomenology*. Once Critical Theory is situated within the perspective of an Hegelian radicalisation of transcendentalism, it can pursue a double design. On a positive theoretical level, it is able to understand knowledge in the essentials of its transcendental configuration as a phenomenon of the process of formation of the human subject. Since this process has an objective social significance, no critique of knowledge is able to ignore it. On a strategic level, Critical Theory thus places itself in a position to clarify its own status in relation to the theory of science of positivism and the contemplative theory in the tradition of first philosophy.

Hegel denounces the Kantian critique of knowledge, which represents knowledge as an instrument or as a medium, in the name of absolute knowledge and with the aim of abolishing epistemology altogether. Nevertheless, it is impossible to ignore the weight of the phenomenological argument which Hegel vindicates against the unacknowledged presuppositions of the critique of knowledge and hence against all abstract epistemological inquiry. The resolution 'never to submit to the thoughts of others on authority, but to test everything oneself and only follow one's own conviction'[16] captures this abstract attitude most adequately. The implications of this attitude must be examined one by one. In his immanent critique of Kant, Habermas brings together these implications in the form of three presuppositions which the *Phenomenology of Spirit* placed in question: the concept of knowledge; the knowing subject; and the Kantian distinction between theoretical and practical reason.

[16] Hegel, *Phänomenologie des Geistes*, Einleitung, p. 67; trans. p. 50.

Kantian epistemology, because constituted at the level of the reflection of an abstract understanding which aspires to be critical, is only apparently free of presupposition. In fact, it presupposes a very specific concept of knowledge and of the knowing subject. Kant grants privileged status to scientific knowledge, that is, the knowledge of the physico-mathematical sciences. The validity of this knowledge is presupposed from the start as prototypal of all knowledge. It is invested with normative force and recognised as the ideal of all knowledge. The critical enterprise of pure theoretical reason therefore 'pre-judges' a specific category of knowledge, the category of knowledge which admits of validation and which can be used to elucidate the organisation of our entire cognitive faculty. The claims of a critique of knowledge which acts at the level of the scepticism of the abstract understanding are placed in question by its uncritical embrace of a science whose criteria provide a yardstick which immediately determines all valuable forms of knowledge. A critique of knowledge which accepts the radicalisation attendant on submission to the rigours of Hegel's 'self-perficient scepticism' is quite different. This critique does not privilege any form of knowledge or set up any as the only valuable form. It seeks to understand all knowledge which appears, including science, as the phenomenal knowledge of a natural or phenomenal consciousness. The process of genesis of this knowledge is reconstructed in phenomenological reflection, but without introducing any predetermined criterion or any yardstick dictated by a normative model. Such a scepticism indicates a questioning or conscious examination of all forms of knowledge without appeal to any external authority in the form of accepted knowledge or opinion, or even to its own authority, in order to establish the truth. Its only claim is conscious and self-reflective insight into the 'untruth' of all knowledge which appears.

Scepticism ... directed towards the entire extent of phenomenal knowledge makes the spirit able to examine what is truth in that it brings about despair with the so-called natural representations, thoughts and opinions which it is indifferent to call its own or alien. The consciousness which proceeds *straight* to the business of examination, however, remains imbued with and bound to these representations, thoughts and opinions and is thus rendered incapable of carrying out its task.[17]

Metacritical reflection which questions the critique of knowledge must therefore contrive an access to the objectified preformations and predeterminations in the world of social life, whereas an abstract epistemological inquiry which naïvely invests scientific knowledge with a privileged, normative status remains blind to this world and to its inherent predeterminations and unconsciously reproduces it. In so far as the *Phenomenology of Spirit* is able to open up this access, Habermas is ready to take over its overall orientation.

The same holds for the second presupposition which underpins the Kantian critique of knowledge: the acceptance of a ready-made concept of the knowing subject, or, more precisely, a normative concept of the Ego. Although the transcendental unity of self-consciousness is conceived by Kant as consequent on an original act of apperception, the identity of this Ego is given in advance by the simple certitude offered by the experience of transcendental self-reflection. From his phenomenological point of view, Hegel observes that the Kantian critique of knowledge assumes a consciousness which is not transparent to itself. Consciousness for Kant does not experience a self-reflection which would enable it to say how it passed from the state of natural consciousness to that of pure self-consciousness on the basis of which the critique of knowledge is developed. Such an experience reveals that the identity postulated for the concept of the subject which initiates the critique of knowledge is only acquired as the result of the process of its formation and in the self-certitude of its appropriation.[18]

---

[17] *Ibid.*, p. 68; trans. p. 50. Habermas, *Erkenntnis und Interesse*, pp. 14–36 esp. p. 23; trans. pp. 7–24 esp. p. 12.

[18] Habermas, *Erkenntnis und Interesse*, pp. 25–36; trans. pp. 15–24.

Finally, Hegel's metacritique advances the concept of phenomenological experience in order to question the third postulate of criticism: the Kantian distinction between theoretical and practical reason. The concept of the Ego presupposed by the critique of pure theoretical reason differs from that presupposed by the critique of practical reason. An Ego understood as unity of self-consciousness differs from an Ego conceived as free will. The critique of pure theoretical reason is therefore separated from the critique of pure practical reason, and this separation seems a matter of course. However, once we understand Hegel's phenomenological experience as a form of reflection which proceeds by *determinate negation*, such a distinction and separation becomes problematic. As we have seen, far from being the empty scepticism of an abstract understanding which sees in its negation only pure nothingness, determinate negation perceives negation as a 'result which contains what is true in the preceding knowledge'. It expresses the continuity between the configurations of consciousness which succeed one another through *Aufhebung* in a way which testifies to the unity between theoretical and practical reason.[19]

This figure of determinate negation does not relate to any immanent logical nexus, but to the mechanism of the progress of a reflection in which theoretical and practical reason are one. The affirmative moment which lies in the negation of an existing disposition of consciousness makes sense when we consider the way in which categories concerning the interpretation of the world are interwoven in this consciousness. A *form of life* which has become an abstraction cannot be negated without trace, it cannot be overturned without practical consequences. The overthrown state is preserved in what is revolutionised because the insight of the new consciousness consists precisely in the experience of revolutionary release from the old consciousness. Because the relation between successive states of a system is produced by determinate negation in this sense, and not by a logical or causal relation, we speak of a process of formation. A state defined simultaneously by cognitive acts and sedimented attitudes can only be overcome in the form of an analytically recollected state. A past state which was simply cut

[19] *Ibid.*, p. 28; trans. p. 18.

off and suppressed would retain its hold over the present state. That relation, however, guarantees continuity to an ethical context of life which destroyed again at each new stage of reflection. Within the sequence of surrendered identifications, it makes possible a continuing identity of 'spirit'. This identity of spirit, which appears to consciousness as a dialectical identity, contains the distinction confidently presupposed by epistemology between theoretical and practical reason *within* itself. The identity cannot be defined in relation to this distinction.[20]

The critical consciousness of Kantian 'epistemology' which is thus replaced by the concept of speculative experience is equally a result of speculative experience. This becomes clear as soon as it is realised that the genesis of its own point of view, considered now as the consciousness of the phenomenological observer, becomes translucent in proportion as the determinations of the process of the formation of consciousness are reconstructed and appropriated. At the end of the *Phenomenology of Spirit* Hegel asserts that this point of view constitutes absolute knowledge. This Habermas contests. His own critique demonstrates the aporias in Hegel, reasserts the importance of a critical inquiry into knowledge and prepares the ground for a transition to Marx.

Absolute knowledge can be contested on the grounds that Hegel is only led to a concept of absolute knowledge as a result of presuppositions borrowed from Schelling's philosophy of identity which suggest the presence of an absolute movement of spirit in its phenomenological experience. There are, moreover, considerable difficulties in integrating the approach of the *Phenomenology of Spirit* with the rest of the Hegelian system, especially the *Science of Logic*. Even if these difficulties are set aside, however, Hegelian metacritique still presents a problem. If we accept the relevance of the phenomenological argument to the critique of knowledge, and if we accept that it constitutes a metacritical radicalisation, must we therefore conclude from this the necessity of

[20] *Ibid.*, pp. 28–9; trans. pp. 18–19.

dissolving all theory of knowledge, all epistemological inquiry, as Hegel does? Habermas claims that the presuppositions of Schelling's philosophy of identity give Hegel's radicalisation of the critique of knowledge an ambiguous status: his metacritique is in the service of an absolute knowledge which seeks to make all critical investigation of knowledge superfluous. If this is the case, what has happened to the relation between philosophy and science? Whereas Kant's critique, which was oriented towards the physical and mathematical sciences of his time, was able to furnish criteria for science as such, Hegel attempts to reveal these criteria through phenomenological experience and ends in absolute knowledge. He must therefore be content with a concept of speculative science.

In relation to this norm, the positive sciences, both natural and human, can only prove embarrassing limitations on absolute knowledge. Consequently, the paradoxical result of this ambiguous radicalisation of the critique of knowledge is that philosophy does not assume an enlightened position towards science. With philosophy's claim to be the true science, the relation between philosophy and science simply vanishes from the discussion. In Hegel there arises a fatal misunderstanding, namely, that to defend the rights of rational reflection against the abstract thought of the understanding means to usurp the rights of the independent sciences in the name of a philosophy which remains the *scientia universalis*. The very fact of scientific progress independent of philosophy must expose this claim, however misunderstood, as a bare fiction. This is the ground on which positivism builds. Only Marx could have challenged its victory. For Marx followed Hegel's critique of Kant, but without sharing the presuppositions of the philosophy of identity which prevented Hegel from achieving an unambiguous radicalisation of epistemology.[21]

3 MARX'S METACRITIQUE

To understand Hegel's *Phenomenology of Spirit* would mean to eliminate the presuppositions which make it a philosophy of identity, and thus to extend its transcendentalism into a

[21] *Ibid.*, p. 35; trans. p. 24.

pragmatic and evolutionist anthropology. This is the view which underlies Marx's metacritique of the critique of knowledge. In his interpretation of Marx, Habermas will maintain that this metacritique produces another form of the dissolution of epistemology, even though it also contains elements of an instrumentalist epistemology. Habermas first identifies the elements in Marx which form an instrumentalist epistemology and indicates the extent to which this remains bound to the transcendentalism of German Idealism. Once he has thus replaced knowledge within the context of the process of formation of the human subject, Habermas then restores the concept of self-reflection in order to justify an epistemology conceived as social theory which avoids the Marxist dissolution of epistemology.

Habermas maintains that Marx reasserts the priority of the concept of nature against the Hegelian thesis whereby nature is simply spirit in its otherness, and thus radically undermines the immanent philosophy of identity in the *Phenomenology of Spirit* and the absolute knowledge that proceeds from it. Marx's rejection of the presuppositions of idealism and of the philosophy of identity as expressed in the *Phenomenology* does not arise so much from a naturalism inherited from Feuerbach as from the social and anthropological import with which he invests the fundamental concept of German Idealism, the concept of action. *Handlung* is understood as production or social labour. Marx places the concept of action within the framework of a theory of evolution which reconstructs the process of formation of man, a creature of nature, in his constitutive relation to first nature, external and irreducible to any spiritual substance. This central category of Marx's anthropology overcomes the naïve naturalism of Feuerbach, rediscovers the positive core in Hegel's idealism and reveals the social and anthropological implications of transcendentalism. Nature which remains external as first nature can only be constituted for us as objective nature through the mediation of the subjective nature of man in the process of social labour. This leads to the conclusion that the concept of labour as deployed in Marx's analyses is not simply a constitutive anthropological category, but also has an epistemological import. The system of action which objectifies nature in itself and the subjectivity of human nature, a system which contains the effective conditions for any possible production and reproduction of social life, furnishes at the same time the transcendental conditions for the possible objectivity of the object of experience and cognition. Hence the concept of labour for Marx functions as a constitutive principle both for the reconstruction of the production and reproduction of social life and for the constitution of the world of the object of cognition.

Man is not only a creature of nature, but he is a human creature of nature, that is, a creature existing for itself, hence a creature of his species, and must confirm himself and act as such in his being and in his knowing. Neither are human objects natural objects as they immediately seem, nor is human sense or meaning, as it immediately and objectively appears, human sensuality. Neither nature objectively, nor nature subjectively is immediately and adequately present to the human creature.[22]

The concept of social labour which this philosophical anthropology seeks to substitute for the Hegelian concept of mediation, reverts in Habermas's eyes, to the Kantian concept of the synthetic activity of the knowing subject. This concept in its new Marxist version may be termed the concept of *social synthesis*. Habermas develops his argument against the theoretical background of analyses taken from contemporary German philosophical anthropology. Arnold Gehlen's theory of evolution is of particular interest on account of the skilful exploitation of the concept of action to illuminate bio-sociological and cultural dimensions while preserving the central position reserved for this concept in the transcendental philosophy of German Idealism.[23] Similarly, Habermas explicates the essential elements of the

---

[22] *Ibid.*, pp. 36–40; trans. pp. 25–8. Marx, Engels, *Gesamtausgabe*, I, 3, vol. I, Berlin, 1932, p. 150.

[23] Arnold Gehlen, *Der Mensch*, Athenäum Verlag, Frankfurt-on-Main, 1962.

concept of social labour in a way which will justify the reinsertion of an epistemological import into Marx's analyses of the concept.

On the basis of the first thesis on Feuerbach[24] it is certainly possible to develop a materialist account of the Kantian concept of the synthetic activity of the knowing subject in terms of the concept of labour. Habermas, however, believes that it is illegitimate to equate labour in this sense with the invariable structures of a life-world (*Lebenswelt*) and hence attempt a definition of the transcendental essence of man on the basis of this concept. An essentialism of this kind which derives from a phenomenological understanding of Marxism[25] is very far from being the concern of Marx. The concept of labour should be placed instead within a theory of evolution of a pragmatist inclination. Labour is a determining mechanism in the process of the formation of man, of man's becoming man. The interest of materialist epistemology in the concept of synthetic activity arises from Marx's metacritique of Hegel's *Phenomenology*. This radicalised the Kantian critique of knowledge, but at a different level of reflection from Hegel. The self-reflection of consciousness developed in the *Phenomenology of Spirit*, instead of leading to a synthesis of subject and object in the absolute movement of the absolute concept, must, if it is to be thoroughly radical, necessarily come up against the original structures of the process of social labour where an instrumental and cognitive synthesis of the subjective nature of man and an objective nature takes place. Although Marx never elaborated the concept of synthesis essential to a materialist epistemology, certain allusions along the lines of the first thesis on Feuerbach make it possible to identify a number of characteristics

---

[24] Marx, *Theses on Feuerbach*, in Marx, Engels, *Gesamtausgabe*, I, 5, p. 522; trans. in *Karl Marx*, ed. T. B. Bottomore and M. Rubel, Penguin Books, Harmondsworth, 1969, p. 82. 'The chief defect of all previous materialism (including that of Feuerbach) is that things, reality, the sensible world, are conceived only in the form of objects of observation, but not as human sense activity, not as practical activity, not subjectively.'

[25] Habermas, *Erkenntnis und Interesse*, p. 40, n. 36; trans. p. 29.

which would distinguish it from the concept of synthetic activity as understood by Kant, Fichte and Hegel.

How does the materialist concept of synthetic activity differ from the transcendental concept? Whereas Kant, Fichte and Hegel were all concerned with some form of logical nexus, the materialist version has no such reference. Synthetic activity for Marx is not a simple act of transcendental consciousness (Kant) or the self-positing of an absolute Ego (Fichte) or the absolute movement of absolute spirit (Hegel). It expresses a dimension which is *both empirical and transcendental* where the acts of the historical human subject in its production and reproduction of social life are understood as the mediation between the subjective nature of man and an objective nature. Whereas Kant, Fichte and Hegel have recourse to the synthesis (the synthesis between subject and predicate), Marx refers us to a concept of *social labour of a socio-economic order*. The critique of political economy may therefore claim the theoretical place occupied by the critique of classical formal logic in transcendental philosophy.[26]

The mediation between the subjective nature of man and an irreducible objective nature can now be located in the historical process of social labour. The mediation does not however express an absolute unity between man and nature. Such a unity is only conceivable on the basis of the philosophy of identity of Hegel's *Phenomenology*. Marx's criticism of this philosophy always insists on the autonomy of a 'prehistoric' nature, a nature *in itself* and *irreducible*, as expressed in his concept of synthetic activity. This insistence fulfils an important epistemological function, namely, 'to hold fast to the contingency of nature and to preserve its brute facticity against the idealistic attempt to dissolve it into the mere otherness of spirit – even though it is embedded in the historical and universal mediating nexus of labouring subjects'.[27]

[26] *Ibid.*, p. 47; trans. p. 34.
[27] *Ibid.*

If one compares the materialist concept of the synthetic activity peculiar to the subjective nature of man with the Kantian theory of knowledge, a certain formal identity may be discerned. Like Kant, Marx maintains the fixed framework of a *subjective disposition* of man in relation to the objectification of all objects of nature. However, this transcendental disposition of Kantian epistemology is reabsorbed in Marx into the theory of instrumental action. That the relation of the human subject to surrounding nature is invariable, is, indeed, a Kantian moment in Marx's analyses. This relation, however, is treated from the perspective of an evolutionist and pragmatic anthropology.

The conditions of instrumental action arose contingently in the natural evolution of the human species. These conditions, however, also bind our knowledge of nature with transcendental necessity to the interest in potential technical control over the processes of nature. The objectivity of experience is constituted within a conceptual schema which is determined by deep-seated anthropological structures of action and which is equally binding on all subjects whose life depends on labour. The objectivity of experience is thus bound to the identity of a natural substratum, namely, the physical organisation of man as disposed to action, and not to an original unity of apperception which, according to Kant, guarantees the identity of ahistorical consciousness as such with transcendental necessity.[28]

In short, Habermas is saying that the Kantian moment in the concept of synthetic activity understood as social labour could have been developed within the discourse of an instrumentalist epistemology. This epistemology would have to explain the transcendental context of the process of social labour, a context where the possibility of experience and of the objectivity of knowledge would be understood from the point of view of an instrumental and technological domination of nature. The idea of the transcendental or quasi-transcendental dimension to human behaviour represented in instrumental action and communicative activity is maintained. This line of thought returns to the possibility

[28] *Ibid.*, p. 49; trans. p. 35–6.

of an epistemology which draws its theoretical strength from the pragmatism of Peirce and Dewey, Konrad Lorenz's anthropology of knowledge, Gehlen's philosophical anthropology and the Hegelian metacritique of Kant's critique of knowledge.[29] The few allusions to such an epistemology which are to be found in Marx are certainly not sufficient to form a developed theory. Nevertheless, they do explain the reasons for Marx's affirmation of the exact natural sciences, an affirmation which was to amount to a form of positivism and which Habermas indicts. A pragmatic anthropological conception of scientific knowledge predominates in Marx although it is never explicitly stated. The production and objectification of scientific knowledge in the process of theoretical research and its application in the production and reproduction of social life constitutes a differentiated extension of an anthropologically constitutive activity which is objectified in social labour. The forms which these objectifications assume in the history of the human subject are contingent and vary according to the level of the social and historical development of man. The identity of the knowing and acting subjects which Kant attributed to an ahistorical transcendental consciousness must consequently be conceived and defined in relation to these objectifications which determine that identity.

Habermas seeks to explain the presence of this non-Kantian moment in Marx's concept of synthetic activity by reference to one of the fundamental ideas in Fichte's *Wissenschaftslehre*. Fichte's idealist critique of the Kantian conception of transcendental apperception as the condition of the possibility of the identity of self-consciousness is translated into the discourse of historical materialism. Fichte, whose speculative argument is based on Kant's practical

---

[29] C. S. Peirce, *Collected Papers*, vols. i–iv, ed. C. Hartshorne and P. Weiss, Harvard University Press, 1931–5; vols. vii–viii, ed. A. W. Burks. Harvard University Press, 1958. J. Dewey, *The Quest for Certainty*, Minton, Balch, New York, 1929; *Experience and Nature*, Norton, New York, 1929; *Human Nature and Conduct*, Holt, New York, 1922. K. Lorenz, *Die Rückseite des Spiegels. Versuch einer Naturgeschichte menschlichen Erkennens*, Piper, Munich, 1973.

philosophy, understands the identity of self-consciousness as an original action (*ursprüngliche Handlung* or *Tathandlung*), or as a self-positing of the Ego which at the same time opposes itself to a non-Ego which is understood as the objectification of a previous unconscious activity and which conditions the Ego: 'In considering your present self-positing which is raised to clear consciousness, you must conceive of a previous such positing which occurs without clear consciousness to which the present self-positing relates and by which it is conditioned.'[30] Habermas explains Marx's analyses in the light of Fichte's speculative schema. It is only by opposing itself to the objectified forms of social production, its non-Ego, and by understanding them as its own products that the subject of social labour can acquire knowledge, form itself, and understand its own identity in its activity. The identity of self-consciousness which Kant conceived of as a *disposition* to a synthetic activity thus appears from this point of view as an *acquisition*.[31] Marx, Habermas asserts, attempts to restrict the domain of unconscious activity of Fichte's Ego to the socio-historical world of the human subject and thus rejects the Fichtean idealism which would have it include the unconscious production of nature itself. In this way, Marx understands the concept of synthetic activity through social labour as a *Selbstsetzung* or *Tathandlung* which is relative to the given stage in the process of the socio-historical formation of man. The synthetic activity effected through social labour presupposes the evolution of nature up to the appearance of hominids. The bio-morphological disposition of hominids marks the transition from nature to culture. This is the evolutionist moment in Marx's anthropology of knowledge which replaces the idealism of an unconscious activity of an Ego or of an absolute spirit.[32]

[30] J. G. Fichte, *Werke*, ed. Medicus, vol. III, p. 109. Habermas, *Erkenntnis und Interesse*, pp. 52–5; trans. pp. 37–40.
[31] Habermas, *Erkenntnis und Interesse*, p. 55; trans. p. 40.
[32] *Ibid.*, pp. 56–8; trans. pp. 40–2.

4 FROM EPISTEMOLOGY TO SOCIAL THEORY

An assessment of the double metacritique directed by Hegel and Marx at the critique of knowledge and transcendental philosophy of German Idealism would be bound to conclude that both must lead to the dissolution of epistemology. In the one case, the philosophy of identity immanent to the *Phenomenology of Spirit* compels the concept of self-reflection to sublimate the Kantian critique in absolute knowledge. In the other case, the reduction of the entire cognitive dimension to the concept of social labour makes all theory of knowledge otiose. This reduction, as is clear in Marx's metacritical appropriation of the *Phenomenology*, ends up by abandoning the concept of self-reflection because it understands the transcendental concept of reflection in terms of the model of production.[33] To the extent that its pragmatic and anthropological assumptions depend on instrumental action, this reduction of the cognitive dimension leads to a capitulation before positivism.

The value of these two metacritiques clearly does not lie in the dissolution of epistemology. The radicalisation of the critique of knowledge undertaken by Marx and Hegel makes it possible to place the problem of knowledge within the context of the process of formation of the human subject without ignoring the social nature of this context. Hence Habermas's thesis: all theory and all epistemology refer to this social context and therefore appeal to a social theory. A reference of this kind does not necessarily entail the elimination of epistemological inquiry as such. How can we appreciate the social nature of knowledge and of its theoretical objectifications in the natural and human sciences without falling into the pitfalls of a sociology of knowledge[34] and without proclaiming all epistemology superfluous? The

---

[33] *Ibid.*, p. 61; trans. p. 44.

[34] Cf. Adorno, 'Das Bewusstsein der Wissenssoziologie', in *Kulturkritik und gesellschaft*, Suhrkamp, Berlin, 1955; 'The Sociology of Knowledge and its Consciousness', in *Prisms*, trans. S. and S. Weber, Spearman, London, 1967, pp. 37–49.

social context to which appeal is made is to be taken in a very wide sense of the term: it does not mean producing a relativist account of the problem of knowledge by hypostasising some absolute social nature. It involves criticising epistemology which ignores the process of the formation of man and the socio-cultural *a priori* immanent to this process. This 'socio-cultural world' is conceived globally. Habermas shuns all 'sociologism'. His thesis intends to enlarge and enrich the concept of the social by extending it to all the manifestations of the human spirit. But how can the Hegelian concept of self-reflection be preserved in order to challenge positivism and in order to decipher and reconstruct the process of formation of the human subject? These are the questions which lead Habermas to his conception of an epistemology as social theory. They intimate that epistemology depends on the elaboration of an adequate concept of the science (or sciences) of man. In order to achieve this, it is necessary to open up a theoretical perspective which attempts once more to give a critical exposition of the respective positions of Hegel and Marx. This perspective appears to be dictated to a certain extent by a neo-Kantian and historicist[35] reading of Hegel's *Phenomenology* and of Marx's *1844 Manuscripts* and *German Ideology*. The pretext for this interpretation is provided by the Hegelian concept of system as developed in the *Jena Philosophy of Spirit*. In this early concept of system an 'historicist' moment and an 'anthropological turn' may be discerned in Hegel's philosophy. Habermas reads these moments into the *Phenomenology* and then proceeds to integrate them into an immanent critique of Marx.

Habermas's essay on the *Jena Philosophy of Spirit* entitled 'Labour and Interaction'[36] argues that the categories *family, tool* and *language* constitute the three fundamental models for

---

[35] Dilthey, *Einleitung in die Geisteswissenschaften*, and *Gesammelte Schriften*, vol. 1; Ernst Cassirer, *Philosophie der symbolischen Formen*, vol. 1, Introduction; cf. especially his remarks on Hegel's *Phenomenology*.

[36] Habermas, 'Arbeit und Interaktion', in *Technik und Wissenschaft als 'Ideologie'*, pp. 9 ff.; trans. in *Theory and Practice*, p. 142.

the dialectical relations which mediate, each in its own way, subject and object, and which designate, respectively, the spheres of *social interaction (Sittlichkeit)*, the *process of labour* and *symbolic representation*. These categories constitute the three *Mitte*, the specific figures of mediation, in which the process of formation of spirit is objectified. In the *Phenomenology of Spirit* Hegel abandoned the concept of system which supported this constellation of figures and developed a form of philosophy of identity.[37] Habermas is interested in this concept of system on account of its recognition of the specificity of the three distinct spheres and of their unique logic and structure. These figures are not subsumed in the single logic of the absolute movement of the self-reflection of spirit. Moreover, in this concept of system, spirit is not defined in terms of the manifestation of the absolute in these objective figures. It is the totality of the dialectical relations of *symbolisation*, the *process of labour* and *social interaction* which define the concept of spirit.[38]

Such a concept of system is doubly valuable from the point of view of the preoccupations with epistemology, historicism and Marxian anthropology which guide Habermas's approach to the *Phenomenology*. First, it admits an epistemological inquiry which, following the methodological concerns of Dilthey, Rickert and Cassirer, remains attentive to the requisite adequation between theory and its object and recognises the specificity of the object as founded in the distinct domains of the formation of spirit.[39] Secondly, it justifies freeing Hegel's *Phenomenology* from the presuppositions inherited from an onto-theological philosophy of identity and opting for the Marxist version. This concept of system preserves the critical and strategically important concept of self-reflection, eliminates the positivist strain in Marx and avoids the descriptivism of neo-Kantian historicist epistemologies.

[37] Hegel, *Phänomenologie des Geistes*, Vorrede, 19; trans. p. 10.
[38] Habermas, 'Arbeit und Interaktion', pp. 10 ff.; trans. pp. 143 ff.
[39] *Ibid.*

In a formal sense, Hegel's *Phenomenology* and the meta-critique contained in the *1844 Manuscripts* and the *German Ideology* can now be understood in terms of the two objective figures of spirit found in the *Jena Philosophy*, namely, *social interaction* and the *process of social labour*. The *Phenomenology* can now be read as the reconstruction of the process of formation of the human subject from the point of view of the anthropologically constitutive domain of *social interaction*. Once the *Phenomenology* has been freed from its metaphysical concept of substance, it is found to relate essentially to the figure of spirit developed in the *Jena Philosophy* under the title of 'ethical relation' (*sittliches Verhältnis*), and hence to the paradigm of social interaction. Moreover, when the presuppositions of the philosophy of identity are abandoned, the other anthropologically constitutive domain in the formation of the human subject is released from the hold of the absolute concept, namely, the process of *social labour* which depends on material praxis and instrumental action. It is this second paradigm which Marx brings into play in his metacritical interpretation of the *Phenomenology*.

> The greatness of Hegel's Phenomenology and its end result – the dialectic of negativity as moving and productive principle – is therefore . . . that Hegel understands the self-production of man as a process, objectification as disobjectification, as alienation and as *Aufhebung* of this alienation; its greatness is that he grasps the essence of labour and understands objective man, man who is true because real, as the result of his own labour.[40]

Marx, as we have seen, understands the process of the formation of the historical human subject essentially in terms of this paradigm. Habermas argues, however, that in this way Marx comes to regard the process of social labour as itself absolute. The dialectical movement of production comes to absorb the entire sphere of praxis as conducted within the framework of communication and social interaction, or, in Hegelian terms, all the forms of phenomenal consciousness.

---

[40] Marx, Engels, *Gesamtausgabe*, I, 3, p. 156. Quoted by Habermas, *Erkenntnis und Interesse*, pp. 59–60; trans. p. 43.

The concept of instrumental action, however, has no power to understand and criticise the sphere where the forms of domination and ideologies are objectified as a set of *relations of production*.

As well as the forces of production in which instrumental action is sedimented, Marx's theory of society also incorporates the institutional framework, the relations of production. It does not ignore the structure of symbolically mediating interaction or the role of cultural tradition. It is only on the basis of these aspects of praxis that domination and ideology can be understood. These aspects of praxis were not, however, integrated into the philosophical foundation of the theory. It is here, where instrumental action cannot penetrate, that phenomenological experience moves. Here, the forms of phenomenal consciousness which Marx calls ideologies appear, and here reifications are dissolved beneath the silent force of a reflection to which Marx restores the Kantian name of critique.[41]

The intention behind Habermas's criticism of Marx is to establish the *irreducibility* of the two paradigms in question – *social interaction*, which includes communicative activity, the struggle for recognition and class antagonisms, that is, ethical and political praxis, and, *labour or social production* through instrumental action, that is, technical and material praxis. Once this irreducibility is established, the question of the theoretical objectifications proper to each domain must be considered. These are, respectively, the human hermeneutic sciences and the exact nomological sciences. The differences between the two become clear once the epistemological inquiry into the foundations of the human sciences is no longer bound, as in positivism, to a model dictated by the physical and mathematical sciences, and is free to find the conditions for an adequation between theory and its object which respects the specificity of the object.

Marx's relation to positivist scientism is ambiguous. The relation of his social theory to the physical and mathematical sciences remains affirmative, because, as we have seen,

[41] Habermas, *Erkenntnis und Interesse*, pp. 58–9; trans. p. 42.

elements of a pragmatic and instrumentalist epistemology
provide him with the theoretical framework for his understanding of the exact sciences which determine production
in industrial society. Marx, moreover, never explicitly
addressed the question of the necessity for a distinction
between the natural and human sciences. What can be discerned, and indeed appears explicitly, is a positivist tendency to subsume and integrate the latter in the former.[42]
Nevertheless, when he considers the status of his own social
theory, Marx understands it as a critique which retains a
normative significance inherited from the practical philosophy of Kant and Fichte. The normative sense of the concept
of critique which belongs to decisive Enlightenment is essential to Marx's social theory. This concept is indispensable if
Marx is to justify his emancipatory intent in a way which
goes beyond the subjective moralism of Kant and Fichte, the
limits and dangers of which he so clearly saw, and if he is to
apply this emancipatory intent in a theoretically coherent
manner to the social totality. Habermas therefore believes
that Critical Theory must integrate a double experience into
this concept of critique: the experience of Hegelian
phenomenological reflection, and the experience of the
epistemology of the human sciences which its founder,
Dilthey, understood as a critique of historical reason which
complements and extends the Kantian *Critique of Pure
Reason*.[43]

The structure and genesis of the relations of production
which are objectified in what Marx calls ideologies can only
be interpreted and elucidated by taking over the model of
reflection from the *Phenomenology of Spirit* in a materialist
form. Ideologies can be understood through the Hegelian
model of reflection in the same way as the configurations of
phenomenal consciousness in the *Phenomenology*. These
configurations which belong within the sphere of social
interaction constitute an objective set of relations of force,

[42] *Ibid.*, pp. 63 ff.; trans. pp. 46 ff.
[43] Dilthey, *Einleitung in die Geisteswissenschaften*.

domination and constraint (class antagonisms, social repression, etc.) and hence a political and institutional framework which, according to Marx, is in contradiction with the system of the forces of social production. A social theory which attempts to understand the process of formation of mankind both by means of the concept of production based on social labour, and in terms of class antagonism, is induced to submit in the first place to the reflective movement of Hegelian experience in order to clarify its own status. A phenomenological reconstruction of the objective configurations of phenomenal consciousness in their dialectical relation with the system of the forces of production is essential to this theory. This dialectical relation which underlies Marx's theory of revolution must in turn be investigated at an epistemological level in order to delineate and found the difference between the paradigms which arise respectively from the sphere of social interaction and the sphere of production through social labour. The importance of this epistemological inquiry is that Habermas can thereby avoid Marx's reductionism by returning to the transcendentalism of German Idealism and to neo-Kantian and historicist epistemology. If the specific realm of social interaction is to be restored to the logic that properly governs it, then, Habermas argues, the concept of synthetic activity, which Marx inherited from Kant but restricted to the single category of material production through labour, must be reexamined and extended. This is the only approach to the dialectical relation between social interaction and the system of the forces of production which is able to understand this relation in a retrospective moment of reflection and to criticise it in a prospective and normative moment with a view to its abolition.[44]

Habermas's intention is to combine the reflective movement of Hegel's phenomenological experience with an epistemological inquiry into the human sciences which is incorporated within Marx's social theory. In this way, he hopes to

[44] Habermas, *Erkenntnis und Interesse*, pp. 76–87; trans. pp. 54–63.

elaborate an adequate concept of the science of man which would make possible a radical critique of knowledge, a metacritique of epistemology, as social theory. But, 'Marx did not develop this idea of the science of man. Indeed, by equating critique with natural science, he repudiated it. Materialist scientism merely confirms once more what absolute idealism had already achieved: the dissolution of epistemology in favour of a universal science freed from its bondage. Here the universal science is not absolute knowledge, but scientific materialism.'[45]

5 THE SELF-REFLECTION OF SCIENCE

The radicalisation of the Kantian critique comes to a sorry end. Hegel capitulates to metaphysics in the claim to be the universal science, and Marx capitulates to its latter-day counterpart, scientistic positivism. It is this that leads Habermas back to Kant. However, Hegel and Marx, in spite of their respective capitulations, opened up the way to understanding knowledge in its process of formation, or as the process of formation of the human subject. It is this theoretical perspective which Habermas exploits when he returns to the Hegelian phenomenological project in a way which does justice to Kant but avoids the aporias of Kantian philosophy. This enterprise clearly requires that due account be taken of the changed theoretical presuppositions. It is thus impossible to continue with Hegelian 'phenomenal knowledge'. Attention must now be directed to the knowledge presented as phenomenal in the positive objective forms of the exact natural sciences and of the socio-historical sciences. The social implications of these forms of knowledge are now at issue.

In the modern world, science harnessed within advanced industrial society has become the decisive factor determining the life of mankind. Nonetheless, in spite of its continual appeals to science, positivism has never subjected science to

---

[45] *Ibid.*, p. 86; trans. p. 63.

a penetrating philosophical interrogation. Science is its idol, its ideal norm. Habermas affirms that positivism, from Comte to the present day, has always signalled the end of epistemology as understood by Kant. Transcendental inquiry into the conditions of the possibility of knowledge, although it set up the model of the physical and mathematical sciences as a norm and as a criterion of true knowledge, was committed to producing an explanation of the meaning of knowledge as such. Positivism, which defines the meaning of knowledge in terms of the results of the positive sciences and explains knowledge of the basis of the methodological analysis of scientific procedures, can find no relevance at all in this kind of philosophical intervention. The transcendental question of the conditions of the possibility of knowledge is consequently reduced to an inquiry into the laws governing the construction and verification of scientific theories. The philosophical question is only seen as meaningful with the terms of this reduction. From this point of view, to leave the sphere of methodology and restore a philosophical epistemology would be to fall back into metaphysics.[46]

Positivism is therefore the end of epistemology. It has replaced the philosophical concern of the latter with theory of science and methodology. According to Habermas, this exchange involves the loss of the concept of the knowing subject and the question of the constitution of the object of knowledge. In the philosophical tradition which runs from Kant to Marx, the knowing subject, in the form of consciousness, the Ego or mankind, was a central point of reference. The transcendental foundations of the knowing subject meant that the validity of knowledge could not be separated from the conditions of its genesis. Contemporary theory of science believes that it can dispense with any such point of reference. The corpus of scientific knowledge is regarded as a given system of rules by reference to which theories can be constructed and verified. As a result of this restriction of

[46] *Ibid.*, pp. 88–91; trans. pp. 67–9.

epistemology to a methodological question, the subjects who follow these rules methodically need not themselves be taken into account in any explanation of the cognitive process.

The obverse of this restriction is that logic and mathematics become autonomous as formal sciences, with the result that the problem of their foundations can no longer be discussed in the context of the problem of knowledge. As a research methodology, the theory of science presupposes the validity of formal logic and mathematics. These in turn are separated off as autochthonous sciences from any dimension where the genesis of their fundamental operations could be made the subject of inquiry.[47]

The problem of the constitution of the object of knowledge (the question of the possibility of experience) is intimately bound to the previous problem in so far as this object results, in Kant's transcendental philosophy, from the synthetic activity of the knowing subject. This, too, is banished from all epistemological consideration because positivism, in the name of its vaunted objectivism, declines to recognise any such activity on the part of a subject. The problem of the constitution of the world vanishes simultaneously. Hence naïve realism. The naïveté is made explicit in the revival of the famous copy theory of truth, based on the isomorphism of image and object, proposition and fact. This point of view forms the basis of its immanent objectivism.[48]

The historical development of positivism since Comte has led to the unlikely position where contemporary theory of science seems to follow in the line of the metacritiques which Hegel and Marx directed against Kantian epistemology. Positivism, it could be said, has assumed their task of liquidating all epistemology. This repression of epistemology has been accomplished so effectively and successfully by contemporary theory of science that it would be vain to attempt an external return to Kant in order to assert the importance of his inquiry and the necessity of surmounting positivism. It is safer strategically to adopt an immanent approach, that is, to follow the internal development of

[47] *Ibid.*, p. 90; trans. p. 68.   [48] *Ibid.*, p. 91; trans. p. 69.

positivism and then proceed to reconstruct it. Because positivism has sought to confine all epistemological problems which it regards as meaningful within methodology, methodology must be reconstructed from within. By bringing the limits of positivism to light it may be possible to transcend these limits and so make possible a self-reflection of science. As we have seen, the very absence of this self-reflection is positivism. This absence has been formally registered in the course of the methodological debate which Critical Theory initiated with contemporary theory of science in relation to the problem of the foundations of the human sciences. This deficiency is to be found throughout the entire history of positivism. Habermas seeks to trace this loss of reflection historically in an outline of the history of positivism since Comte. He concentrates on two authors whom he regards as exemplary in that they seem to point the way to a genuine self-reflection of science. These authors are Peirce and Dilthey. These two contemporaries of nineteenth-century positivism prepared the ground for the self-reflection of science by the way in which they pursued their respective methodological inquiries into the logic of scientific research and the foundations of the human sciences. Neither explicitly achieved this self-reflection, but they discovered an interest at the heart of scientific knowledge. Moreover, they succeeded in showing the extent to which this interest was bound to the objective context of social life.

Habermas's interpretation of Peirce and Dilthey emphasises the constitutive elements of human behaviour which are manifested in the irreducible paradigms of *instrumental action* and *communicative interaction*. The exact, nomological sciences and the socio-historical, hermeneutic sciences are concerned respectively with the two spheres to which these two paradigms refer. The historicist and neo-Kantian presuppositions which enshrine the difference between these two types of science underlie Habermas's attempt to describe these sciences and the paradigms on which they are based. Research in the analytico-empirical sciences is a methodical extension of a cumulative process of apprenticeship which was carried out at a pre-scientific level within the functional framework of instrumental action (material praxis). The socio-historical or hermeneutic sciences transmit to us a knowledge which depends on a process of understanding developed and objectified at a pre-scientific level in social interaction guided by communication through linguistic symbols. In the case of the natural sciences, we can speak of the production of knowledge of technical value since they relate to the theoretical project of the control of nature. The hermeneutic sciences only produce a practical knowledge which depends on social interaction. They seek to guarantee intersubjective understanding.[49]

Within the functional framework of instrumental action, we constitute our objective world from the point of view of the technical control of nature. In terms of the Kantian co-ordinates of Habermas's thought, this means on the basis of the transcendental conditions of the synthetic activity of the theorising subject, that is, the research scientist. This perspective of instrumental action clearly involves a restricted concept of language and experience. Language is understood here in its instrumental function, in its capacity for formalisation, while experience is reduced to controlled observations. The concept of language which corresponds to instrumental action remains essentially *monologic*, as opposed to communicative interaction, where the structure is essentially *dialogic*. In this case, reality is constituted within a form of social life where social groups communicate through the medium of ordinary language and within a framework which structures interaction as grammar structures ordinary language games. This reality which is the object of inquiry in the hermeneutic sciences already exhibits a transcendental structure which the theorising subject, that is, the interpreter or hermeneut, finds as given.

The object domain in the human sciences is not constituted only under the transcendental conditions of the methodology of

49 *Ibid.*, pp. 235–43; trans. pp. 191–7.

research [as is the case in the natural sciences – G. K.]; it is found as already constituted. Certainly, the rules of every interpretation are laid down by the model of symbolically mediated interactions. However, once the interpreter has been socialised in his mother tongue and trained to interpret, he does not move *among* transcendental rules, but *at the level* of the transcendental conditions themselves. He is only able to decipher the experience contained in an historical text in relation to the transcendental structure of the world to which he himself belongs. Theory and experience do not diverge here as they do in the empirical and analytical sciences. Whenever a communicative experience which is reliable within the common schemata of understanding and action breaks down, interpretation must be brought into play. This interpretation is directed both at the experience acquired in the world constituted by ordinary language, and also at the grammatical rules for constituting this world. It is both linguistic analysis and experience at once. Similarly, in obtaining a consensus between antagonists, interpretation modifies its initial hermeneutic anticipation of consensus by a consensus achieved through mutual recognition of grammatical rules. Here, too, experience and analytical insight converge.[50]

Peirce and Dilthey developed the methodology of the natural and human sciences as a logic of scientific research. Peirce emphasised the pragmatic *a priori* of an experience which arises in instrumental action towards objects of nature. Dilthey emphasised the *a priori* of an experience which arises in communicative interaction as mediated through language. Both came to understand the process of scientific research within the horizon of an objective context of life. The logic of scientific research thus regains a genuinely epistemological dimension in which the restoration of a form of transcendentalism may also be discerned. In spite of their reference to Kant, Peirce and Dilthey in no way return to a philosophy of consciousness which would claim to offer an answer to the problem of the possibility of scientific knowledge or the possibility of understanding an historical object. It is the merit of these two authors, in Habermas's eyes, that they eschew all reference to a solipsistic or

[50] *Ibid.*, pp. 238–9; trans. pp. 193–4.

monologic consciousness, and direct their attention to the pragmatic *a priori* of the process of scientific research (Peirce), or to the *a priori* of an objectified form of life (Dilthey). It may certainly be conceded that the philosophical foundations of their methodological inquiries are debatable. Peirce preaches the realism of universals,[51] and Dilthey borrows a concept of life from German Idealism.[52] Nevertheless, the special status of their work is guaranteed by the reference in the one to the pragmatic context of life defined by instrumental action, and, in the other, to a form of life which is preformed in communicative interaction. This distinguishes it from logical positivism and from Kantian transcendental philosophy. Drawing on the phenomenological analyses of 'life-worlds', Habermas seeks to invest his own work with an analogous status so that he may finally broach the question of the interest of scientific knowledge.

The immanent logical investigation of progress in the empirical-analytical sciences and of the process of hermeneutic explication soon comes up against limits. Neither the status of the modes of inference which Peirce analysed, nor the circular movement of interpretation which Dilthey uncovered are satisfactory from the point of view of formal logic. How induction or the hermeneutic circle are 'possible' cannot be shown logically, but only in epistemological terms. Both cases concern rules for the logical transformation of propositions whose validity (*Geltung*) only makes sense if the propositions transformed are related *a priori* to determinate categories of experiences within a transcendental framework, whether of instrumental action or of a form of life constituted through ordinary language. These systems of reference have a transcendental function, but they determine the structure of research processes and not the structure of transcendental consciousness as such. Unlike transcendental logic, the logic of the natural and human sciences is not concerned with the structure of pure theoretical reason, but with the methodological rules for the organisation of research processes. These rules no longer have the status of pure transcendental rules. They have a transcendental function but arise from the factual contexts of life: from the structures of a species which reproduces its life through learning proces-

[51] *Ibid.*, pp. 116–42; trans. pp. 91–112.
[52] *Ibid.*, pp. 143–233 and pp. 262 ff.; trans. pp. 113–86 and pp. 214 ff.

ses of socially organised labour and through processes of understanding in interactions mediated by ordinary language. The sense
of the validity (*Sinn der Geltung*) of statements which can be derived
within the quasi-transcendental systems of reference of the
research processes of the natural and human sciences is therefore
to be measured against the context of interests of these underlying
relations of life. Nomological knowledge is technically useful in the
same sense that hermeneutic knowledge is practically effective.[53]

This reference to the transcendental framework of the
nomological sciences and of the hermeneutic sciences in
order to explain the 'sense of the validity' of their respective
cognitions simply expresses a phenomenological and historicist reaction to the Kantian concept of 'consciousness as
such'. In Habermas's case, this reaction arises from a
materialist and anthropological interpretation of the
Hegelian concept of subject, understood as the historical
human subject, and of its process of formation, which is
substituted for the Kantian transcendental consciousness.
Within the context of this process, the phenomenological
concept of 'life-world' and its *a priori* structures has a transcendental function. This *Lebenswelt* stands as a transcendental point of reference behind the two anthropologically constitutive configurations in the process of formation of the
historical human subject – labour and interaction, or
instrumental action and communicative interaction. This
world also forms the point of reference for the theoretical
inquiries which arise within these two configurations: the
nomological sciences guided by a technical cognitive interest
and the hermeneutic sciences guided by a practical cognitive
interest. These sciences in turn predetermine and direct the
orientation of research or the modality of cognition. If the
concept of cognitive interest is given a naturalistic and
biological interpretation, or if it is understood in a psychological sense, or attributed wholly to the transcendental sphere,
or wholly to the empirical sphere, then cognition will never
be understood adequately. Habermas defends the concept of
cognitive interest against these one-sided interpretations

[53] *Ibid.*, pp. 239–40; trans. pp. 194–5.

and underlines the necessity of preserving the peculiar status of the concept. It is both empirical and transcendental, and cannot be reduced to simple psychological considerations, or to simple cognitive and logical considerations.[54]

Peirce and Dilthey stumbled on the interested origin of knowledge while elaborating their respective logics of scientific research. Neither, of course, developed a concept of cognitive interest, or reflected sufficiently on the relation which binds knowledge to interest. To have done so, they would have had to traverse theoretical terrain which would have seemed very strange to them, or even appeared as a return to metaphysics. They both stood firmly on the ground of positivism, and could only have succeeded in going beyond its narrow limits if they had been able to introduce an epistemological dimension into their methodological thinking. They would, in effect, have had to call upon the Marxist version of the Hegelian concept of the process of formation of the historical human subject. Although they prepared the way for a self-reflection of science, neither Peirce nor Dilthey succeeded in clarifying the full import of his own work.

If they had been able to do so, they could not have resisted that experience of reflection which Hegel unfolded in the *Phenomenology*, the experience of the emancipatory force of reflection which the subject experiences in itself as it becomes transparent to itself in the history of its own genesis. The substance of the experience of reflection is articulated in the concept of the process of formation. This experience leads methodically to a standpoint from which reason becomes identical with the will to reason.[55]

[54] *Ibid.*, pp. 241–2; trans. p. 196.   [55] *Ibid.*, pp. 243–4; trans. p. 197.

5

The practical perspective of Critical Theory and its aporias

From a strictly Hegelian point of view, to attribute a prospective and normative import to the Hegelian concept of self-reflection, and to turn the entire theoretical structure of metacritique on this concept, as Habermas does, is to relapse into the philosophy of reflection which defined Enlightenment for Kant and Fichte. It is also to relapse into the moralising subjectivism which Hegel never tired of attacking and questioning.[1] Although he fully recognises that he remains bound to this philosophy of reflection at a theoretical level, and is fully aware of its aporias, Habermas restores the stratagem of Enlightenment for practical ends. The issue at stake is the very *raison d'être* of philosophy. In spite of his experience of the aporias which have been discussed,[2] Habermas employs a concept of Enlightenment which extends beyond the limits of its historical definition to cover the very concept of philosophy itself. Philosophy is in essence Enlightenment, in the sense that its concept of truth is pre-eminently a reflective experience of the false pursued with a view to emancipation from the constraints of untruth. Having challenged the complacent claim to neutrality espoused by all contemplative theory which ignores praxis, Habermas posits emancipation as the *telos* of philosophy. The identification of philosophical theory with emancipation forms the core of his argument. It is this that compels

[1] Hegel, *Glauben und Wissen, Erste Druckschriften*, ed. G. Lasson, Meiner, Leipzig, 1928; *Faith and Knowledge*, trans. W. Cerf and H. S. Harris, New York Press, Albany, 1977.

[2] Cf. chapter 2 above.

him to subject self-reflection to his concept of emancipatory cognitive interest, in accordance with his critical reception of the theories of Kant, Fichte and Marx. The effect of this is to transfer the ends of Enlightenment to the level of practical discourse.[3]

This leads Habermas to outline a theory of communicative competence centred on the idea of a universal pragmatics. Its task is to diagnose the splitting of symbols which occurs when speech is subjected to systematic distortions. In addition, by operating counterfactually, it is to provide the rules for constraint-free communication. It presents a remarkable resemblance to the model of psychoanalysis. What status does Habermas accord to Freudian psychoanalysis, and how does he define his universal pragmatics in relation to it?

I FREUD'S METAPSYCHOLOGY AND UNIVERSAL PRAGMATICS

Habermas approaches Freud's metapsychology in the light of Hegel's *Phenomenology*. In this way, he is able to discern in Freud an experience of reflection. Positivism, operating at the level of abstract scientistic understanding, forgot and repressed this reflection. The methodological inquiries of Peirce and Dilthey into the scientific research which constituted that understanding were only able to indicate the possibility of a self-reflection, without being able to accomplish it. Paradoxically, Freud's psychoanalysis, nurtured in the bosom of positivism, and aspiring to the status of an empirical science, constitutes a form of scientific self-reflection. The essence of Freud's analytic technique is to detect unconsciously motivated forms of constraint in human behaviour and to overcome them in the process of therapeutic work. This gives Freudian analysis a peculiar

---

[3] Habermas, *Theorie und Praxis*, 3rd edn, Einleitung; trans. pp. 1 ff. Cf. also 'Vorbereitende Bemerkungen zu einer Theorie der kommunikativen Kompetenz', in *Theorie der Gesellschaft oder Sozialtechnologie?*, p. 101.

status which distinguishes it from the interpretative processes of the hermeneutic sciences and from the scientistic logic of positivism.[4]

It is tempting to regard psychoanalysis in a general way as an interpretative technique which relies on the hermeneutic category of understanding in order to gain access to a context which depends on communicative interaction through linguistic symbols. It seems to have the same object as the philological hermeneutic sciences. Closer examination, however, reveals that it goes beyond all established hermeneutics by introducing a new dimension into the object of investigation and, consequently, a new dimension into its mode of treatment.

It is certainly possible to discover formal resemblances between approaches used by Freud and those employed by the founder of hermeneutics in the human sciences, Dilthey. References to biography and to the critical reconstruction of a distorted context may be found in both writers, but the theoretical perspectives of the two approaches are quite different. Dilthey's choice of biography as a model for successful understanding of historical life was determined by a theory based on the irreducibility of the concept of life. Biography is able to make an historical life transparent. As the historical life comes to light in the immediate act of recollection on the part of the author, in the act of autobiography, there can be no resistance from any source of opacity. For Dilthey, life is 'that which is known from within, it is that which precludes further regress'.[5] For Freud, in contrast, biography is an object of analysis only in so far as it constitutes both the known and the unknown, and impels analysis to go beyond explicit recollection to question what is not said.[6] Dilthey, like Freud, recognises the necessity for a critique of immediate subjective memory. In the act of biographical recollection, memory is entrusted with

[4] Habermas, *Erkenntnis und Interesse*, pp, 262 ff.; trans. pp. 214 ff.

[5] Dilthey, *Gesammelte Schriften*, vol. VII, p. 261. Habermas, *Erkenntnis und Interesse*, pp. 264 ff.; trans. p. 215.

[6] Habermas, *Erkenntnis und Interesse*, pp. 264 ff.; trans. p. 215.

guaranteeing the meaning of subjective intentions or presumptions, even though the hermeneutic understanding as such must be directed towards the historical context of a form of objective spirit. The philological criticism adduced at this point to restore a text corrupted by the defects in subjective biographical memory is of an essentially different nature from the reconstructive critique of psychoanalysis. In philological and hermeneutic criticism, the ultimate criterion is still the reference to a *conscious* subjective intention and its concomitant concept of meaning, however much the historical context of a form of objective spirit is taken into account. It is this criterion which guides the critical reconstruction of the corrupt text, guarantees its meaning, and is responsible for eliminating all deficiencies. Psychoanalytic interpretation is not concerned with the context of a conscious intentionality. On the contrary: its critical labours are not devoted to making good defects, eliminating accidental deficiencies, but to giving a systematic meaning and importance to what is missing, to what fails to appear.

The omissions and displacements have a systematic function, for the symbolic contexts which psychoanalysis seeks to understand are vitiated by *internal influences*. The corruptions have meaning *as such*. The meaning of a corrupt text of this kind can only be satisfactorily understood once the meaning of the corruption itself has been explained. This is the specific task of an hermeneutics which is not limited to a philological approach, but which unites linguistic analysis with psychological investigation of causal contexts.[7]

Psychoanalytic interpretation is therefore concerned with a context of communication through symbols in which evidence of a latent content may be found, beyond the manifest and explicit content of the text, which points to a different meaning. Failures of memory, errors in writing or reading, which are regarded by philological hermeneutics as external accidents, have an internal origin. Psychoanalysis regards them as indices of the presence of this meaning which eludes the subject in question although intimately bound to it.

[7] *Ibid.*, p. 266; trans. p. 217.

Moreover, this *Tiefenhermeneutik*, this hermeneutic task which Habermas attributes to psychoanalysis, is distinct not only from the historicist tradition of philological hermeneutics, but also differs from contemporary philosophical hermeneutics.[8] However much this latter may claim a radicality deriving from the fundamental ontology of understanding, it remains dominated by the assumptions of ordinary language, by the communicative competence which these assumptions nourish, and by the notion of meaning they promote. Where distorted speech or distorted communication arises, psychoanalysis is able to discover a meaning at an entirely different level from that of ordinary language. A case such as this would be excluded from hermeneutic inquiry which would regard it as beyond the reach of its understanding, and reject it as pathological.[9]

The object of psychoanalysis is thus attended with a host of signs, symbols and gestures which seem incomprehensible to us. They seem incomprehensible for the sole reason that they do not obey the regular norms of the grammar of ordinary language and its paradigms for communication, that is, they represent deviations from the models established by a socio-cultural tradition. Freud takes these digressions and deviations into account and designates them by the term of symptoms. He understands them to be the results of compromise between repressed desires of infantile origin and social prohibitions which prevent the realisation of those desires. Symptoms are substitute satisfactions, they express both the frustration and the social sanction. They are therefore ultimately

signs of a specific self-estrangement of the subject in question. The breaks in the text testify to the force of an interpretation produced by the self, yet strange to the Ego. Because the symbols which the repressed needs interpret are excluded from open public communication, *the communication of the speaking and acting subject with*

---

[8] Gadamer, *Wahrheit und Methode*. Habermas, 'Der Universalitätsanspruch der Hermeneutik', in *Hermeneutik und Ideologiekritik*, Suhrkamp, Frankfurt-on-Main, 1971, pp. 120 ff., especially pp. 133 ff.

[9] Habermas, 'Universalitätsanspruch', pp. 134 ff.

itself is in turn interrupted. The privatised language of unconscious motives is cut off from the Ego, although internally it is deeply affecting the use of language and the motivation of actions controlled by the Ego. As a result, the Ego necessarily deceives itself about its identity in the symbolic structures that it consciously produces.[10]

In a context such as this, a renewed comparison of hermeneutic interpretation and psychoanalytic interpretation is required in order to define the characteristics of the latter more closely. In the case of philological hermeneutics, the interpreter is generally concerned to establish communication between interlocutors speaking different languages or belonging to different eras. He seeks to institute an intersubjective understanding by eliminating difficulties due to differences in cultural context and socio-historical determinations. He always proceeds within the limits of ordinary language games and their grammatical norms. This model cannot apply to the psychoanalytic object for a very simple reason: in pathological cases, indeed, in cases such as communication between analysand and analyst, the communication is not distorted in a direct way, but in an indirect way, through the influence and limitations of symptoms. Moreover, in his everyday life, that is, in the customary conditions of social repression, the neurotic endeavours to maintain intersubjective understanding, employing the mechanisms of ordinary language games and following the directives of social sanctions. But

the price he pays for undistorted communication under these circumstances of frustration is *distortion of communication within himself*. If the illusion of intersubjective constraint-free communication is not to be diminished, then the restrictions on public communication necessary under the institutional relations of control must be set up within the subjects themselves. Thus the *privatised section of excommunicated language* is reduced to silence in the person of the neurotic, along with the undesirable motives of action, and made inaccessible to him.[11]

---

[10] Habermas, *Erkenntnis und Interesse*, pp. 278–9; trans. pp. 227–8.
[11] *Ibid*., p. 279; trans. p. 227–8.

This distortion of communication requires an interpreter who does not mediate between interlocutors of different languages, but who teaches one and the same subject to understand his own languages.

The analyst instructs the analysand to read his own texts which he himself has corrupted and displaced, and to translate the symbols from a mode of expression which has been deformed in a private language into the mode of expression of public communication. This translation opens up the genetically important phases of his life history to recollection that was previously blocked, and makes him conscious of the process of his own formation. To this extent, psychoanalytic interpretation, unlike the hermeneutics of the human sciences, is not concerned with understanding symbolic configurations as such. The *act of understanding* to which psychoanalysis leads *is self-reflection*.[12]

Everything that Habermas takes from Freud is organised around this fundamental thesis. The connection with Hegel's *Phenomenology* is beyond doubt. In both Hegel and Freud a truth is to be uncovered from the experience of the false in a kind of *self-Enlightenment*. In Hegel, this appears as the reflective recollection which converts the configurations of phenomenal consciousness into true knowledge where consciousness becomes transparent to itself.[13] In Freud, this appears in the form of the hypothetical constructions of analysis which release a self-reflective process of recollection destined to produce a translation of the unconscious into the conscious, to convert the Id into the Ego.

Freud, of course, conceives his enterprise as a positive empirical science. The natural sciences are the model for all his theoretical constructions as well as for analytic therapy. He always regarded it as imperative that they should have the rigour of an analytic and causal explanation. It is not easy to see, however, how the entire psychoanalytic project could be subjected to the paradigm of the natural sciences

---

[12] *Ibid.*, pp. 279–80; trans. p. 228.
[13] Hegel, *Phänomenologie des Geistes*, Einleitung, p. 75; trans. p. 56. 'as consciousness drives towards its true existence, it will reach a point where it lays off its illusion of being bound to what is strange, to what is only for it and as an other ...'

and their principle of causality. If there is a question of any kind of causality within a psychoanalytic context, then it cannot be the causality found in events of nature. It could only be the causality of second nature, in the Hegelian sense of the term. The young Hegel explicated this as the causality of fate, having in mind a context of loss and restitution in a domain of life.[14] The question then arises whether Freud mistook the nature of his own enterprise. Does not psycho-analysis, both as a theory and in praxis, develop a logic which transcends the limits of an empirical science and its causal thinking? According to Habermas, Freud's thought does suffer from this misunderstanding. Freud asserts, for example, that the progress of psychoanalysis depends on the exact realisation of a programme conceived on the model of the positive empirical sciences. On account of his scientism he was unable to define the status of his theory or to under-stand adequately the metapsychology to which it referred. It was this scientism which also prevented him from under-standing his thought as a universal interpretation of the processes of formation oriented towards Enlightenment.

Freud may well have surmised that the realisation of the pro-gramme for a 'scientific', or even strictly behaviourist, psychology would mean sacrificing the one purpose to which psychoanalysis owes its existence: the purpose of Enlightenment, whereby the Id is to become Ego. Nevertheless, he did not abandon that programme. He did not understand metapsychology in the only way possible from the point of view of self-reflection: as a *universal interpretation of processes of formation*.[15]

Such then is the task which Habermas wishes to confer on psychoanalysis. Metapsychology would have the status of a logic of interpretation, making possible the analysis of a pathological context of ordinary language and interaction. By drawing attention to the corresponding determinations in their transcendental frameworks,[16] methodological self-

[14] Habermas, *Erkenntnis und Interesse*, pp. 312 and 330 ff.; trans. pp. 256 and 271 ff.
[15] *Ibid.*, p. 309; trans. p. 254.
[16] *Ibid.*, pp. 310–11; trans. pp. 254–5.

reflection in the natural and human sciences was able to reveal, in the one, a specific instrumental context of language and action, and in the other, a context of language and intercommunication. Metapsychology, in turn, discloses and reflects on a linguistic context which is equally fundamental: the context of distorted communication and pathological behaviour.

Metapsychology thereby presupposes a theory of ordinary language. The task of this theory is to explain the intersubjective validity of symbols and the linguistic mediation of interactions on the basis of reciprocal recognition, and to show how socialisation into the grammar of language games can be understood as a process of individuation. Since, according to this theory, the structure of language determines language and praxis to an equal extent, motives of action are also understood as linguistically interpreted needs. Motivations are not occult instincts, but intentions which are subjectively regulating, symbolically mediated and reciprocally limiting.[17]

Habermas draws on the work of Alfred Lorenzer,[18] which treats the analysis of dynamic instinctual processes as a linguistic analysis within the framework of a *Tiefenhermeneutik*, in order to confer a similar task and status on Freud's metapsychology. Once more, this *Tiefenhermeneutik* is contrasted with philosophical hermeneutics, and is seen to bring into question the latter's claim to universality. Philosophical hermeneutics cannot support such a claim, Habermas asserts, as long as it fails to consider the limits of its fundamental category of understanding. These limits are made clear by psychoanalysis, which is concerned not only with the pathological, but also with what appears as normal. By going beyond the limits of hermeneutics, psychoanalysis brings its underlying assumptions into question:

What hermeneutics regards as self-evident can only be shaken when it is shown that the model of systematically distorted communication reappears in 'normal' speech, that is, in speech which

---

[17] *Ibid.*, p. 311; trans. p. 255.
[18] A. Lorenzer, *Sprachzerstörung und Rekonstruktion. Vorarbeiten zu eine Metatheorie der Psychonanalyse*, Suhrkamp, Frankfurt-on-Main, 1970.

is not noticeably pathological. This can be shown in the case of pseudo-communication where the distortion in communication is not perceived by those concerned. It is only the outsider who notices that the one is misunderstanding the other. Pseudo-communication engenders a system of misunderstandings which remains impenetrable because of the illusion of consensus. The lesson we have learned from hermeneutics is that, as long as we move within a natural language, we cannot step outside the role of the actors who are the object of reflection. We therefore have no universal criterion which would allow us to determine whether we are caught in the false consciousness of a pseudo-normal understanding, or whether we are regarding something that is in reality in need of systematic explanation simply as a difficulty which can be disposed of by normal hermeneutic measures. The limits of hermeneutics are to be found in the fact that we discover systematically produced misunderstandings as such – without initially 'understanding' them.[19]

To understand systematic misunderstandings and to overcome them in an analytic and reflective way, it is necessary to merge the theoretical perspective of psychoanalysis with the horizon of philosophical hermeneutics. However, to transform hermeneutics in this way into a meta-hermeneutics necessarily presupposes a theory of communicative competence.

This is what Habermas seeks to elaborate on the basis of the concept of a universal pragmatics. The prime function of a universal pragmatics is to furnish the rules which would make it possible to diagnose the splitting of symbols in speech subjected to systematic distortion and to achieve a true consensus in a constraint-free speech situation. Meta-hermeneutic reflection, which aims to develop a normative Enlightenment, then seeks to elucidate the dogmatic core of philosophical hermeneutics, namely, the idea of the primacy of an ontological pre-understanding as the horizon of all consensus.

Insight into the structures of prejudice which are presupposed in all understanding of meaning is no justification for identifying the

---

[19] Habermas, 'Universalitätsanapruch', in *Hermeneutik und Ideologiekritik*, p. 134.

consensus actually achieved with true consensus. Indeed, this identification leads to an ontologising of language and hypostasising of tradition. A critical, enlightened hermeneutics which is able to distinguish between insight and delusion must incorporate the meta-hermeneutic knowledge concerning the conditions of the possibility of systematically distorted communication. It must bind understanding to the principle of rational discourse whereby truth would only be guaranteed by the lasting consensus reached under idealised conditions of communication free from constraint and domination.[20]

The anticipation of a communication free from constraint, founded on the projection of an ideal speech situation, replaces the normative orientation of the critical reason of the Enlightenment. This idea contains the conditions for the application of the concept of the emancipation of man from objective constraints whose hold is witnessed by the very fact of distorted communication. This also makes it possible to define the status of the meta-theoretical discourse necessary for the elaboration of the concept of a universal pragmatics.

The key to the argument ironically presupposes an unexpected return to the neo-Kantian understanding of the meaning of Kant's transcendental inquiry, a return to the *quaestio quid juris*. Heidegger's fundamental ontology and Gadamer's philosophical hermeneutics claimed to have eliminated this question as a consequence of the ontological primacy accorded to the concept of understanding.[21] Habermas, most certainly, does not share the intentions of neo-Kantian epistemology. By means of Kant's *quaestio quid juris*, neo-Kantian philosophy sought to sublimate the meaning of the genesis of all knowledge through reference to an abstract concept of function in which it located the conditions for the validity of knowledge. Habermas returns to the Kantian question of right with the intention of critically questioning the assumptions behind a context of

[20] *Ibid.*, pp. 153–4.
[21] Gadamer, *Wahrheit und Methode*, pp. 240–90; trans. pp. 225–74. Heidegger, *Sein und Zeit*, §§ 31, 32, 33.

communicative interaction and the claim to validity of all discursive theoretical statements which neglect to examine their presuppositions in relation to normative rationality. The meaning given to validity (*Geltung*) in response to the Kantian question of right establishes a kind of tribunal of discursive argumentation before which rationality may be vindicated. This rationality presupposes a communicative competence on the part of the participants, that is, a facility for applying the system of the generative rules of the language. Moreover, this rationality can only be realised in the general structures of a dialogue situation through speech acts. Habermas therefore attributes to universal pragmatics the task of reconstructing the system of rules which make dialogue possible. This reconstruction draws on Chomsky's generative grammar and Searle's speech act theory.[22] As a theory of communicative competence, universal pragmatics emphasises the performative force of ordinary language by analysing the transformation of the basic grammatical unit (the sentence) into the basic unit of dialogue, the speech act or utterance. The regulative canons of communication are therefore shown to be (a) the model of an ideal speech situation which operates counterfactually and makes it possible to diagnose the splitting of symbols in distorted communication, and (b) a consensus theory of truth which questions the dogmatic core of theories of truth founded on isomorphism or the *adaequatio*. When philosophical hermeneutics rehabilitates the structures of prejudice as the presupposition of all understanding of meaning and of all consensus, it perpetuates, *nolens volens*, the concept of truth as *adaequatio*.[23]

The table of fundamental categories which allows a systematic classification of speech acts forms the foundation of a universal pragmatics. This table of categories provides the framework for the identification of the conditions of a

[22] Habermas, 'Vorbereitende Bermerkungen zu einer Theorie der Kommunikativen Kompetenz', in *Theorie der Gesellschaft oder Sozialtechnologie?*, pp. 101–41.
[23] *Ibid.*

true consensus, as well as for locating pseudo-consensus. The 'transcendental deduction' of these categories is guided by the presupposition of the ideal speech situation. The ideal speech situation, one might say, fulfils the function of Kant's transcendental Ego in its constitutive and regulative aspects. However, as the context is no longer that of Kant's mono-logic knowledge, but that of communicative or dialogic understanding, it is effectively the concept of hermeneutic circle which appears in the form of the ideal speech situation. The concept of ideal speech situation has no more than a strategic function. It avoids the dogmatism associated with recognition of the hermeneutic circle. It inherits the function of constitutive principle which devolved on that circle, but does not explicitly restate the requirement of the hermeneutic circle whereby all understanding presupposes an ontological pre-understanding.[24] It requires, instead, a recognition that each act of communication anticipates an ideal speech situation, that each participant in communication presupposes that his interlocutors also move within this ideal speech situation, and that these presuppositions, mutually attributed by all interlocutors, form the conditions of the possibility of communication, and, at a discursive or argumentative level, the conditions for obtaining a true consensus. According to Habermas, this anticipation is brought into play in every speech act. The investigation of the fundamental categories which make possible the articulation of the various aspects of each speech act, and the various classes of these acts, prepares the way for a consensus theory of truth.

If we disregard the first category of speech acts which Habermas designates as *communicativa*, concerned essentially with situating the pragmatic sense of speech (such as 'to say', 'to question', 'to reply'), and examine the category of *constativa* (such as 'to assert', 'to explain', 'to deny', 'to doubt', 'to contest'), then we see that this category of pragmatic universals leads us to introduce the distinction between

[24] The status of the circle nevertheless remains ambiguous.

being and illusion (*Sein und Schein*). These pragmatic universals allow us to make affirmations in the form of propositions
and then to question the truth of these propositions. The
fundamental question which arises in this context is: What
are the regulative conditions governing predication, that is,
for attributing a predicate to a subject in a proposition? In
the tradition of classical ontology and in the implicit ontology of contemporary analytical philosophy, the response to
this question involves reference to the concept of adequation
between knowledge and its object, or to the isomorphism
between the proposition and the fact which the proposition
describes in asserting its existence. Habermas regards this
answer as inadequate for the simple reason that the concept
of correspondence which underlies it must in turn be
explained by other propositions. The same holds for the
concept of actuality (*Wirklichkeit*) which this answer implies,
and its equivalents: the concepts of object or fact. 'Ultimately, the only meaning that we can give to the term
"actuality" is the meaning we imply in true propositions
about existing states of affairs. We are unable to introduce
the concept "reality" (*Realität*) independently of the term
"true proposition".'[25] Only a consensus theory of truth is
able to provide an answer to this question which does not
repeat the ontological circle in a non-ontological way.

According to this theory, I may only attribute a predicate to an
object if every other person who could *possibly* enter into dialogue
with me would attribute the same predicate to the same object. In
order to distinguish true propositions from false, I take account of
the judgement of others ... The condition for the truth of propositions is the potential agreement of *all* others.[26]

In this potential agreement and approbation, references to
the concept of competence and the concept of rationality are
essential. The reference to a straightforward competence

---

[25] Habermas, 'Verbereitende Bemerkungen', p. 124. On the difference between
the truth of the proposition and the truth of the utterance, see Vincent Descombes,
L'inconscient malgré lui, Collection 'Critique', Minuit, Paris, 1977.

[26] Habermas, 'Vorbereitende Bermerkungen', p. 124.

which includes or supports a theoretical rationality (in the sense of knowing how to deal with an object) proves in turn insufficient. Competence must, on the contrary, be supported by a concept of rationality which is placed in the practical context and which consequently relates to a practical discourse which could justify and explain competence. As this practical discourse lies in a different dimension from that of empirical theoretical propositions (which are objects of verification), so its criterion of truth must relate to veracity in a different dimension from the *truth* of *propositions*.[27] 'The utterances of a speaker are veracious if he deceives neither himself nor others.'[28]

The speech acts which arise from the category of *representativa* (such as 'to know', 'to wish', 'to promise', 'to pretend') are concerned precisely with the veracity of utterances. This class of pragmatic universals allows the introduction of the distinction between *essence* and *appearance* (*Wesen und Erscheinung*). What are the conditions which guarantee the veracity of these utterances? Habermas's answer turns to the practical and moral implications of the specific speech act implied. The speech act of promising, for example, implies that the speaker contracts an obligation, and introduces into intersubjective communication the sense of duty. The speaker makes it known through his utterance that he recognises the validity of a normative prescription, the necessity of following a rule of action.

In order to decide the *veracity of utterances*, we refer to the *rightness of actions*. 'To follow a rule' means, in a general sense, 'to act', whether we are concerned, as in social action, with recognised norms, or, as in arithmetic, with constructive rules, or, as in speech, with grammatical rules or the rules of universal pragmatics. Whether someone follows a rule correctly, or whether he intentionally deviates from the rule and makes systematic errors, or whether his behaviour is irregular and therefore guided by no rules at all, is not a question of the truth of propositions or of the veracity of utterances, but a question of the rightness of actions. The rightness of an

---

[27] *Ibid.*, p. 131.   [28] *Ibid.*, p. 131.

action is measured in terms of whether it falls within the set of all the cases permitted by an underlying rule.[29]

The speech acts which belong to the class of *regulativa* (such as 'to warn', 'to advise', 'to forbid', 'to require') relate to such a context of regularity. These pragmatic universals permit a distinction between *is* and *ought* (*Sein und Sollen*). As acting subjects, we are able to determine on the basis of these pragmatic universals, in any given speech situation, whether an event arises from a simple empirical causal regularity or whether it depends on an intentional practical regularity. Once more, however, another question arises: What are the conditions that must be fulfilled in calling an action correct or right in a speech situation? or, On what authority can we judge and verify an action in such a situation?

In order to verify the rule competence of an actor, the rule competence of a verifier is required. But, since neither party can claim any methodological priority over the other, as is the case with the observer and his object, the question whether the actor is following a rule, and the reciprocal question, whether the verifier is able to take over the role of the actor, can only be decided in the last analysis on the basis of a consensus between the two subjects.[30]

Within the language game of a socio-cultural form of life this consensus is easy to attain. One has only to refer to the socio-cultural presuppositions which support this consensus. Once these presuppositions have been questioned, however, consensus can only be established by means of discursive and argumentative procedures which presuppose a certain distance from the practical context. Nevertheless, even if it is the case that reference to consensus in the form of traditional language games or discursive argumentation is inevitable and indispensable, no independent criterion for distinguishing between true and false consensus has been identified. The discussion of the table of the categories of pragmatic universals to which the speech acts in question are

[29] *Ibid.*, p. 133.   [30] *Ibid.*, p. 140.

subordinated produced no such criterion, even if this discussion prepared the way for obtaining a true consensus.

The idea of true consensus demands that the participants in a discourse be capable of distinguishing between being and illusion, essence and appearance, and is and ought, in order to be able to judge competently the truth of propositions, the veracity of utterances and the rightness of actions. In none of these dimensions, however, are we able to name a criterion which would allow an independent judgement on the competence of possible judges, that is, independently of a consensus achieved in a discourse. The judgement of competence to judge must in turn appeal to a consensus, for the evaluation of which criteria were supposed to be found. Only an ontological theory of truth could break out of this circle. None of these theories, however, has as yet survived examination.[31]

When confronted with this aporia, we cannot avoid returning to the guiding presupposition of the argument which has just been expounded. Thus, we may close the hermeneutic circle presupposed at the start of the argument: the presupposition of the ideal speech situation which, as we have seen, has a constitutive and regulative function and which supports the concept of a universal pragmatics. In order to attain a true consensus and uncover untruth through discursive argumentation, or simply in order to engage in communication, we always anticipate an ideal speech situation. As a norm, this situation operates counterfactually. This makes it possible to diagnose distorted communication and to bring about Enlightenment at the level of practical discourse. The double movement of reflection which reappears this time in the context of communication therefore presupposes the ontological implications of the hermeneutic circle which refer to the ideality of a pre-existing (*a priori*) consensus. Habermas avoids discussion of these implications to escape the danger of falling back into the dogmatism of the hermeneutic tradition. However, since the fundamental concepts of Habermas's metacritique, namely, the experience of reflection and its associated philosophical discourse,

---

[31] *Ibid.*, p. 135.

culminate in a reference to this idea of consensus, this meta-critique must be defined philosophically and the limits of its concept of Enlightenment shown.

2 THE LIMITS OF ENLIGHTENMENT

By placing Critical Theory in its philosophical context, I have endeavoured to show throughout this essay that its metacritique was indebted to the Hegelian concept of speculative experience. This debt remained however much Critical Theory intended to make its critique more radical or to express a consciousness of the failure of speculative experience. In the aftermath of Marx and historicist and neo-Kantian epistemology, the principal critical argument cited against this Hegelian concept involves a rejection of the presuppositions which Hegelian ontology inherited from Schelling's philosophy of identity. This philosophy transforms the idealist prejudice of Western metaphysics into a principle: identity is elevated into a transcendental principle. *Subjectivity* is posited as consciousness in order to establish the unity of theoretical and practical reason which eluded Kant in the *Critique of Judgement* in his inquiry into the unifying foundation of the concept of nature (theory) and the concept of freedom (praxis).[32] In the course of the development of transcendental philosophy, this identity gave rise to Fichte's concepts of action and intellectual intuition, and was united via Schelling with Spinoza's concept of substance. It ultimately dictated the form of the entire Hegelian system as the dialectical unfolding of the absolute concept. In particular, it was responsible for one of the most fundamental figures of his practical philosophy, *Sittlichkeit* (objective morality), which is understood as the achieved unity of theoretical and practical reason in the realisation of the idea of the good.[33]

[32] Kant, *Kritik der Urteilskraft*, Introduction §3.
[33] In Hegel, the organisation of the *Encyclopaedia* and of the *Philosophy of Right* testifies to this unity of theoretical and practical reason, a unity which refers to the *Science of Logic*.

We have seen how Critical Theory defined this disposition in Hegel. It denounced his contemplative reconciliations as an ideology which transfigures the antagonistic structure of social reality. The negative dialectic which Critical Theory opposes to Hegel's philosophy can do no more than anticipate, through the reflective experience of its determinate negation, the unity of theory and praxis as the realisation of the idea of the good, and that in a normative sense, as the result of the experience of the false. It is this correction of Kant's practical philosophy, inspired by left-wing Hegelianism,[34] which Habermas proposes in his consensus theory of truth. The idea of the unity of theoretical and practical reason conceived in terms of Schelling's principle of identity cannot be accepted in a way which endorses the ontological prejudice of a pre-established harmony. This unity is only to be achieved prospectively through practical discourse. However, the attempt to relegate the unity of theory and praxis into a prospective dimension runs the constant risk of falling into Kantian moralism and perpetuating the bad infinite which includes the subjectivism of *Sollen*. That this moment is present in the very structure of Critical Theory cannot be in doubt. The importance and originality of Habermas's work, however, lies in his interpretation of the consequences of Kant's practical philosophy: the idea of the primacy of action or praxis which is constitutive for all theory. We have seen how the radicalisation of this Kantian idea by Fichte came to found the unity of theoretical and practical reason on the primacy of the latter – on the primacy of this *Handlung* which the act of self-reflection (reflection on reflection or intellectual intuition) made manifest. Self-reflection has been shown as the speculative foundation of Critical Theory. The unity of theory and praxis which this reflection reveals is now to be understood as an integration of Marx with Fichte: *the necessity for philosophical theory to become practical*. The identity of theory and praxis can only be achieved through praxis, that is, through action which is

[34] Cf. M. Theunissen, *Gesellschaft und Geschichte*, de Gruyter, Berlin, 1969.

revealed by the same token as the presupposition of the identity.[35]

Habermas's appeals to Kant, Fichte and Marx to free him from the dogmatic burden of this principle of identity are to no avail. He remains no less dominated by it. His philosophical discourse turns on this identity. In the retrospective orientation of his reflection he endeavours to make the subject which supports the identity transparent by decoding the forms of constraint to which it is bound. In the prospective and normative orientation, he inquires into the necessary conditions for a practical discourse which could restore a shattered identity. Once Habermas's philosophical discourse has been freed from the dogmatic moment governing the application of the principle of identity, this principle can be used in two ways: first, to develop a metacritique of all epistemology which ignores its own presuppositions, and secondly, to restore a philosophical dimension to epistemology which would make it possible for an adequate theory of the science of man to be developed as social theory. In the first case, the argument draws on Hegel's *Phenomenology* and the philosophical hermeneutics of Heidegger and Gadamer. In the second case, the argument draws on historicist and neo-Kantian epistemology. All critique of knowledge, all epistemology presupposes knowledge: such is the fundamental argument of Hegel's metacritique. According to Kant's transcendental philosophy, knowledge is only possible in a harmony of the faculties guaranteed by the supreme principle of all synthetic *a priori* judgements which express an *identity* between the conditions of the possibility of experience and the conditions of the possibility of the objects of experience.[36] The consequences of this transcendentalism must be made explicit. This is what Hegel does. Habermas is in an even better position to employ this argument since the structure of Hegel's argument is repeated in Heidegger's *Daseinsanalytik* and in Gadamer's philosophical hermeneutics, both

---

[35] Cf. M. Riedel, *Theorie und Praxis im Denken Hegels*, pp. 216 ff.
[36] Kant, *Kritik der reinen Vernunft*, pp. 212–13; trans. p. 194.

of which are metacritiques of neo-Kantian epistemology. This time, of course, the question relates to the problem of understanding. The critical argument, broached from a metacritical point of view, may be expressed as follows: all critique of understanding, all 'critique of historical reason', presupposes understanding. Dilthey formulates the fundamental question of the epistemology of the human sciences in a Kantian manner: How is understanding possible? or, more specifically, How can the historical object be understood? His answer relies on a fundamental category of German Idealism: the concept of life. This concept assumes the role and function of Kant's principle of all synthetic *a priori* judgements. Understanding of the historical *object* by the hermeneutic epistemological *subject* is only possible if one presupposes an *identical* structure in the object and subject of understanding. This structure is manifested in the concept of life. 'Only life understands life.'[37] Heidegger, who attempted to show in his analysis of *Dasein* that understanding constitutes the mode of being of *Dasein*, was able to reabsorb this residue from the philosophy of identity present in Dilthey into the hermeneutic circle of *Geworfenheit* and *Entwurf* where the category of understanding is operative. In this way he could proceed to a metacritical dissolution of all epistemology. Gadamer's philosophical hermeneutics addressed the hermeneutic circle from an Heideggerian perspective in order to apply it to the various configurations of Hegel's objective spirit. Gadamer repeats the same metacritical moment when he seeks to rehabilitate the prestructure of understanding which language, texts, and the various forms of objective spirit incorporate in a predetermining manner.[38]

The speculative tradition which runs from Hegel to philosophical hermeneutics is founded on the principle of identity. This includes all the forms of existential hermeneutics which sublimate the tradition in the claim to have

[37] Dilthey, *Gesammelte Schriften*, vol. VII.
[38] Gadamer, *Wahrheit und Methode*, pp. 205 ff.; trans. pp. 192 ff. See also Foreword to Second Edition.

dissolved it by overcoming metaphysics. This speculative tradition has equal hold over Habermas's metacritique. However, Habermas's return to this tradition subjects the concept of experience and discourse found in Hegel, Heidegger and Gadamer to scrutiny and questioning. It is necessary, in effect, to do as Hegel did, and draw the consequences of Kant's transcendentalism. This means to assert against the critique of knowledge that this critique, which is also knowledge, presupposes a form of phenomenal knowledge of natural consciousness. This, however, need in no way involve a return to absolute mediation of subject and object, spirit and nature, etc. Nor need this imply that the Self (*Selbst*) must be declared identical with itself in the becoming of the absolute concept as experience which elevates the discourse of the speculative proposition to absolute knowledge, thereby affirming the prejudices of phenomenal knowledge. For their part, Heidegger and philosophical hermeneutics emphasised the ontological pre-understanding which is present in all critique of understanding. But, does this argument necessarily imply that the contingent historical prejudice which this pre-understanding inevitably incorporates must be endorsed? Why must we regard this reproduction of the hermeneutic circle of *Geworfenheit* and *Entwurf* as another form of Hegelian speculative experience, 'an experience of being' whose discourse remains dictated by this prejudice, and serves only its legitimation – even if the constraints imposed by metaphysics and by Hegel have been neutralised by the *contingency* of *Dasein*?

In conformity with the tradition of Critical Theory, the arguments which Habermas advances are concerned to question speculative experience and the dogmatic discourse which supports it. From a metacritical point of view, the contribution of Hegel, Heidegger and Gadamer retains an heuristic and regulative value in the Kantian sense of the term. As we have seen, it allows Habermas to proceed to a reconstruction of the process of formation of the human subject, the human species in its contingent social and historical conditions. The actions of this subject have a 'structure' which is simultaneously empirical and transcendental. The objectified forms of these actions are to be investigated in a way which does justice to their diversity, and subjected to a critique which operates counterfactually on the basis of a regulative and normative idea of reason. Historicist and neo-Kantian epistemology is important in the sense that it renewed the Kantian epistemological inquiry and broke with the metaphysical tradition of substance. By lending an epistemological status to the ontological presuppositions of transcendentalism (the principle of identity), it introduced a theoretical margin of manoeuvre where, in combination with an interpretation of Hegel, Marx and the hermeneutic tradition, the idea of an epistemology as social theory could be adumbrated. Moreover, it opened the way to a theory which, by reflecting on the objective forms of the process of formation of the human species on the basis of a practical *a priori*, might in turn open the way to a *praxis*, that is, action guided by an idea arising from an interest in emancipation. The movement of reflection which supports this new experience of reflection is the experience of transparency and the imperative to restore identity. Its affinity with the Kantian idea of the fact of reason (*factum rationis*) is manifest throughout.[39] The source of Habermas's schemata of theoretical construction lies in Fichte's radicalisation of the primacy of Kant's practical reason. It is therefore appropriate to return to this source to identify and locate certain aporias.

In the First Introduction to the *Wissenschaftslehre*, Fichte established a distinction between two kinds of 'immediate determinations of consciousness' or 'representations'. Some, he wrote, appear to us as entirely dependent on our freedom, while others appear to exist independently of us. In relation to the first, we feel that our imagination, our will, appears to us as free, but, in relation to the second, we do not experience this freedom, and, consequently, we feel ourselves bound in the act of cognition to their content. Fichte concludes, 'In

[39] Habermas, *Erkenntnis und Interesse*, pp. 367–417.

short, some of our representations are accompanied by the feeling of freedom, others by the feeling of necessity.'[40] On the basis of this idea of freedom it proves unreasonable to ask 'Why are the representations dependent on freedom determined in one way and not another? . . . they are thus because I have determined them thus, and if I had determined them otherwise, they would have been otherwise.' However, the question 'What is the foundation of the system of representations accompanied by the feeling of necessity, and what is the foundation of this feeling of necessity itself?' is regarded as worthy of reflection.[41]

The task of philosophy is to answer this second question. The importance accorded to this question arises from Fichte's major preoccupation which inspired the entire *Wissenschaftslehre*. It may be formulated as follows: man can only realise his freedom and autonomy if he can secure theoretical and practical control over his own objectified activities, and if he can re-establish hegemony over his own unconscious productions which appear as subject to a blind mechanism, and to follow a regularity of their own which is almost autonomous. Such are the determinations of consciousness which are bound to the 'feeling of necessity'. The idea that these objectified products (the non-Ego) have a 'regularity of their own' takes us to the core of all theories centred on the famous category of alienation (for Fichte, dogmatism). This Fichtean idea functions as a paradigm for the systems of Schelling and Hegel and for the elaboration of Marx's critique of political economy. Their various works give the idea historical application. The Freudian theory of the unconscious also follows this paradigm, even if psychoanalysts are not cognisant of the fact.[42]

The entire theoretical enterprise of Fichte's *Wissenschaftslehre* should be read as an attempt to destroy the autonomy of

[40] Fichte, *Erste Einleitung in die Wissenschaftslehre.*
[41] *Ibid.*
[42] Arnold Gehlen has drawn attention to the relation between Freud and Fichte in an article entitled 'Über die Geburt der Freiheit aus der Entfremdung', which appears in *Studien zur Anthropologie und Soziologie*, pp. 232 ff.

this non-Ego, understood as the totality of the objectified products of an absolute Ego. However, the task of bringing about this form of speculative experience and making all those products absolutely transparent by means of intellectual intuition was only a theoretical enterprise in Fichte's eyes. The conjunction of action with this theory led to his well-known Jacobinism. Hegel carries out an identical programme in the *Phenomenology of Spirit*: this time, Fichte's 'infinite reflection of self-consciousness' is to be sublimated in a determinate negation of each stage of its phenomenal knowledge. On the one hand, the hermeneutic and cathartic experience in which this sublimation is realised leads to an absolute knowledge, a form of self-Enlightenment. On the other hand, it leads to recognition and appropriation of the totality of all phenomenal cultural configurations. Marx projects the same Fichtean idea into an economic infrastructure. In the context of the totalising advent of industrial society, this produces the ultimate form of negation, indeterminate negation *par excellence*, total revolution.

If we remember that the abolition of the Fichtean non-Ego has remained the goal of all these radical philosophical experiences, and if we disregard the speculative extravagances which accompanied Fichte's idea – to be left only with his concept of the autonomy of social institutions – then we may well ask to what extent this non-Ego is the cold destiny of humanity, but also to what extent it may be a source of abreaction of affects and a source of freedom.[43] It is perhaps in this destiny that Enlightenment and the idea of freedom may find their limits. But the experience of industrial and technological society also demands that we question what is to be understood by 'limits'. The technical means at the disposal of contemporary civilisation are capable of continually displacing the limits drawn by the objective forms of social life or institutional forms. Moreover, the process of unfettered production in which our industrial society is engaged has brought about an inevitable disintegration of

[43] *Ibid.*

traditional forms of life and liquidation of their products. When we take cognisance of the fact that the margin separating 'real possibilities' and 'abstract possibilities', to revert to Hegelian terms, appears to be increasingly narrowed,[44] do we not have reason to expect that our societies will become increasingly fluid and, in a certain sense, utopian? If this is the case, how can we establish or institutionalise coherent practical discourse on such fleeting objective ground? How can we realise the idea of a consensus achieved in communication free from constraint and expect from this any coherence of human action when the social and institutional bases of action seem uncertain? Faced with theoretical options which have been tried and outstripped by the consciousness they attained of their aporias, Habermas proposes Enlightenment. Those who embrace these options are reduced to professing a cynical realism, or forced to surrender to the ludism of the aesthete. The dialectic of Enlightenment and the negative dialectic which it presupposes have made these various theoretical attitudes sufficiently transparent. The argument in favour of a practical discourse which Habermas proposes would presuppose a reflective experience of social and political relations. As a critique, his argument seeks to take the place of ideological discourse in a pragmatic and affirmative manner. This theoretical enterprise can therefore have no pretension to possess the *truth*. It is intended as an invitation to a debate.

[44] Hegel, *Wissenschaft der Logik*, vol. ii, pp. 169 ff.; trans. pp. 541 ff. In the tradition of Western metaphysics, the important category of *possibility* has implied a sense of *limitation* and has thereby defined the limits of what can be realised. In industrial technological society this sense is lost. Cf. my article, 'Le sens du possible', in *Critique*, March 1978, no. 370, pp. 303–23.

Jack ⟶ Levy

434-7298

school teacher

Pam Essman

576 - 1807

store 355-5800

Index of names